Heinemann EXPLORE Science

Student Book

New International Edition

Grade 4

Tara Lievesley, Deborah Herridge
Series editor: John Stringer

ALWAYS LEARNING

PEARSON

Pearson Education Limited is a company incorporated in England and Wales having its registered office at Edinburgh Gate, Harlow, Essex, CM20 2JE.

Registered company number: 872828

www.pearsonglobalschools.com

Text © Pearson Education Limited 2012
First published 2003. This edition published 2012.

16 15 14 13 12
IMP 10 9 8 7 6 5 4 3 2 1

British Library Cataloguing in Publication Data
A catalogue record for this book is available from the British Library

ISBN 978 0 4351 3358 0

Edited by Janice Curry
Designed by Scout Design Associates
Original illustrations © Pearson Education Limited, 2003, 2009, 2012
Illustrated by Rosie Brooks, Beehive Illustration Ltd
Cover photo © Science Photo Library Ltd
Picture research by Louise Edgeworth
Indexed by Indexing Specialists (UK) Ltd
Printed and bound in Malaysia, CTP-KHL

Acknowledgements
The publisher would like to thank the following for their kind permission to reproduce their photographs:

(Key: b-bottom; c-centre; l-left; r-right; t-top)

Alamy Images: Aleksandr Ugorenkov 43, B W Flowers 62r, CuboImages ssl 74br, DW Images 37, F Bettex Mysterra.org 75b, Gary Roebuck 94tr, Glyn Thomas Photography 73, Jochen Tack 19, Justin Minns 35, Manor Photography 53tr, Mark Boulton 40, Tim Gainey 75, Wildlife GmbH 32l; **Brand X Pictures:** Joe Atlas 100; **Comstock Images:** 49; Corbis: Ocean 48; **Creatas:** 30, 73tr; **Glow Images:** 104, PhotosIndia.com 17, Tetra Images 22c; Imagestate Media: John Foxx Collection 94br, Paul Goldstein 14, 32; **Pearson Education Ltd:** Trevor Clifford 61, 83tr, 83bl, 86t, 86cl, Coleman Yuen 85, Photolink. Photodisc 87tr, Trevor Stevens 105; **PhotoDisc:** 24tr, Getty 13tl, John A Rizzo 58cr, Lawrence M Sawyer 21bl, Photodisc / Stock Trek 12br, R Morley 95, Sozaijita 38tr, Stock Trek 69; Photos.com: Jupiter Images 24bl; **Science Photo Library Ltd:** A J Photo 18bl, BSIP,Chassenet 18tr, John Reader 6tr, Mehau Kulyk 76, Michael Donne 78, Sheila Terry 25; **Shutterstock.com:** Anette Linnen Rasmussen 45, Anton Derevschuk 94cl, Archana Bhartia 12cl, Armin Rose 22br, Beboy 60, Clive Watkins 58tl, Czintos Odon 33, Denis Nata 72bl, Dmitry Pistrov 80, Elen Studio 101, Gregory Johnston 58bl, Henrik Larsson 29, HLPhoto 74cl, Jan Bussan 66tr, Kuehdi 8, Ninell 53bl, Patrick Poendi 22cl, Rob Marmion 38, Rsooli 36, Terekhov Igor 68, Vahamrick 66bl, Vinicius Tupinamba 71, Vladru 86, Wim Claes 34tr, Worradirek 34bl, Yai 6bl

All other images © Pearson Education

In some instances we have been unable to trace the owners of copyright material, and we would appreciate any information that would enable us to do so.

Every effort has been made to trace the copyright holders and we apologise in advance for any unintentional omissions. We would be pleased to insert the appropriate acknowledgement in any subsequent edition of this publication.

Contents

How to use this book iv

Unit 1: Humans and animals **1**
Animal bones 2
Broken bones 4
Growing bones 6
Your skeleton 8
Contracting muscles 10
Exercising muscles 12
Drugs as medicine 14
Unit 1: Review 16

Unit 2: Living things in their **17**
environment
Different habitats 18
Grouping living things 20
Using keys 22
Investigating invertebrates 24
Food chains 26
Changing habitats 28
Our environment 30
Unit 2: Review 32

Unit 3: Keeping warm **33**
Feeling hot 34
Measuring temperature 36
Hot and cold places 38
Keeping cool 40
Investigating insulators 42
Conducting heat 44
Unit 3: Review 46

Unit 4: Separating solids and liquids .. **47**
Properties of materials 48
Solids and liquids 50
Changing materials 52
Separating materials 54
Heating and cooling 56
Dissolving solids 58
Unit 4: Review 60

Unit 5: Gases around us **61**
Solids, liquids and gases 62
Air around us 64
Air in the soil 66
Different gases 68
Moving gases 70
States of matter 72
Unit 5: Review 74

Unit 6: Electricity **75**
Simple circuits 76
Investigating circuits 78
Conductors and insulators 80
Designing switches 82
Brighter bulbs 84
Magnets and metals 86
Unit 6: Review 88

Unit 7: Sound **89**
Making sounds 90
How sound travels 92
Muffling sound 94
Pitch and volume 96
Changing pitch 98
Different instruments 100
Unit 7: Review 102

Checklists **103**
Unit 1: Humans and animals 103
Unit 2: Living things in their environments ... 104
Unit 3: Keeping warm 105
Unit 4: Separating solids and liquids ... 106
Unit 5: Gases around us 108
Unit 6: Electricity 107
Unit 7: Sound 109

Glossary 110

Index 114

How to use this book

Unit 3: Keeping warm

What do you wear to go to the beach? How does the sea feel after you've been playing in the Sun? Do you want hot soup or ice cream? What happens to the ice cream if you don't eat it fast enough? Would it happen if you kept the ice cream in a freezer?

What do you know?

- Materials have many different properties.
- Some materials have similar properties.
- Some properties are more useful to us.
- Some materials are good electrical conductors of heat and some are good insulators.

Skills check

Can you...
- read a ruler accurately?
- use a computer for your work?

Words to learn

Celsius
conduct
degrees
heat
insulate

insulation
temperature
thermal
thermometer

Let's find out...

Not all countries are hot. In cold countries, the **loft** can be the hottest part of the house. Thats because heat rises. Heat can escape through the roof and the will get house cold. A layer of soft, **fluffy** material is put in the loft to keep the house warm. This material is called loft **insulation**. What would be a good material to slow down the escape of heat? Will a house in a cold country get warm if there is no heating?

At the beginning of each Unit there is a list of things you should already know or be able to do.

Think about these questions. By the end of the Unit you will know how to answer them.

This shows words in the Unit that are important. Learn and use them.

Try these activities. Your teacher will help you.

This box tells you what the lesson is about.

Feeling hot

Things to learn
- Temperature is a measure of how hot or cold things are.
- A thermometer measures temperature.
- Our senses are not accurate thermometers.

Sense of...

How many senses do you have? Where are they found in your body? You have at least five senses – touch, taste, sight, hearing and smell. You have eyes, ears, a nose and a mouth. The sense of touch is also found all over your body. What do you use for sensing **heat**? Can you smell heat or see it? Can you hear it?

Which sense do you use to tell the flame is hot?

Feeling hot

When you are ill, an adult may feel your forehead. They may say you 'have a **temperature**'. They mean that you are warmer than usual. A high temperature may mean you are not well. But touching your forehead does not give an accurate temperature reading. A **thermometer** can measure how hot you are. Normally your body temperature should be 37°C. This means that on a thermometer with a **C**lsius scale, your temperature reads 37. Some thermometers have a Fahrenheit (F) scale. Your temperature should be 98.4°F.

What temperature should the thermometer read if the child is well?

Things to do

Heat sense

How do you know if something is hot? If it is safe, you may feel it. You use your sense of touch. Is this good enough?
- Put one hand in a bowl of hot tap water. Put the other in a bowl of cold iced water. Keep them there for two minutes.
- Then put both hands into a bowl of water at room temperature.
- Describe what you feel.

I wonder...

Thermometers are filled with a dye liquid they look red, green or blue. Some older thermometers are filled with **mercury**. Why is this no longer used?

Dig deeper

Find out:
- about different kinds of thermometers
- if medical thermometers that change colour with temperature are accurate.

Did you know?

- The first thermometer was invented five hundred years ago by the **astronomer** Galileo Galilei.
- The first medical thermometer was made in 1867.
- Thermometers work because the liquid in them **expands** or contracts until it is the same temperature as the surroundings. This can be measured on a temperature scale.

These boxes give you some fascinating facts.

Find out what coloured words in bold mean in the Glossary at the back of the book.

This box tells you what you will find out during the lesson. Your teacher will help you.

Keeping cool

Your challenge
- Use a thermometer carefully and accurately.
- Investigate the best way to keep ice lollies cold.
- Explain what you found out.
- Communicate your conclusions to others.

I could keep them in the cardboard box they are packed in.

I could take off my socks and put the lollies inside them

I could put one in my hat to keep the Sun off it.

I could run with them.

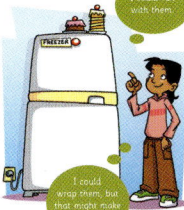

I could wrap them, but that might make them warmer.

I could put one in my pocket to shade it from the Sun.

What to do
Farida has got ice lollies for her friends. She has to take the ice lollies to her friends before they **melt**. Will insulation keep the lollies cold and? What would you do?

What you need
- A thermometer
- A stopwatch
- Ice lollies
- Pieces of different fabrics.

What to check
Now try it yourselves.
- What will keep the ice lollies cold?
- Why does the starting size of each ice lolly matter?
- How will you measure how well the lollies keep?
- How will you measure the temperature of your ice lollies?

What do you find
Each lolly was 16 cm long when Farida took them from the freezer.

Farida measured how long her lollies were when she took them to her friends. These are her results.

Method of insulation	Length of lolly (cm)
in socks	12
in a hat	13
in cardboard	14
in pocket	11

- Draw a graph of her results.
- Which insulation insulation kept the lollies from melting best? How can you tell?
- What was happening to the lollies?
- Draw a graph of your own results. What sort of graph can you draw? Use a computer to draw your graph as well.
- Which insulation kept the ice lollies frozen longest?

Can you do better?
- Farida measured the length of her lollies to see which melted the most. What other measurement could she have taken?
- Did you use a thermometer? How often did you take the temperature of the ice lollies?

Now predict
- If you wrapped different ice lollies in different thicknesses of newspaper sheets, which lolly would stay frozen longest?
- What is the newspaper doing?

Use what you have learned to answer these questions.

Unit 3: Review

What have you learned?
- Temperature is a measure of how hot or cold things are.
- A thermometer measures temperature accurately.
- There are different kinds of thermometers.
- Objects gain or lose heat until they reach room temperature.
- **Thermal** conductors allow heat to travel through them easily and quickly.
- Thermal insulators slow the movement of heat.
- Air is a good thermal insulator; thick fabrics trap air.
- Metals are good thermal conductors.
- How to use a thermometer carefully and accurately.
- You must handle a thermometer with care.

Find out more about...
- wool and why it is used for clothes
- **molecules** cooling down.

Check-up
Maalik takes lunch to school every day. He keeps his lunch box in his classroom. The classroom is warm and there is no fridge. What could he do to keep his lunch cool?

How can Maalik keep his lunch cool?

The answer!
Remember the first question? Loft insulation is very thick with loose **fibres**. It looks like cotton wool. It has air trapped in it. Air is a good thermal insulator. The trapped air helps to insulate the house. The heat that has risen to the loft can't easily escape from the house. This makes it warmer indoors!
If the house isn't warm, then there isn't any heat to keep in. Loft insulation only keeps in the heat that is already there.

Check what you have learned.

Here you find answers to important questions.

Unit 1: Humans and animals

What would we be like without bones? We would not be able to stand – or move! Our **skeleton** supports and **protects** us; it gives us a way to move and keep upright. It doesn't stay the same size. It grows with us. If it didn't we would never grow taller than a baby.

What do you know?

- You can name some parts of your body.
- We need to eat to grow and be healthy.
- As we get older we grow bigger.
- Humans are a type of animal.

Skills check

Can you...

- compare observations that you make?
- decide what to investigate and collect the evidence?
- say what your evidence means?
- communicate what you have found out to others?
- decide whether what you have found out supports your predictions?
- use a ruler to measure length?

Let's find out...

If you break your leg, a doctor puts a plaster cast on it. When the cast comes off, your leg is often thinner than it was. Why does the doctor put the cast on? Why is your leg thinner? How have the muscles changed? What can you do to make both legs look the same again?

Animal bones

Things to learn

- Humans are a type of animal.
- We have a bony skeleton inside our body.
- Some other animals also have a bony skeleton inside them.

These bones all come from a human skeleton

Your bony friend

Feel your hand and fingers. They are soft, but inside you can feel a hard frame. This is part of your skeleton. Without your skeleton you would be a big, shapeless jelly. Your bones keep your shape. Without them, you could not move. They grow with you, getting harder as you get older.

A crab has a skeleton (its hard shell) outside its body

Bones on the outside?

You can find **shells** on the beach. Once, each shell had an animal living in it. The shell was its skeleton. It protected them. These animals had their skeleton on the outside of their bodies. What would we look like if our skeletons were outside our bodies?

Bones are alive!

Inside us our bones are alive and growing. Under the hard shell of your bones are lots of tubes carrying blood to your bones. The insides of bones are filled with air spaces. These make them light and **spongy**.

Big and small

We have many different-sized bones in our bodies. The smallest bone is in our ears. It is called the stapes. It is less than half a centimetre long. The longest is our thigh-bone. This is called the femur. It can be about 60 cm long in an adult.

Things to do

I've got one too!

Our bones are inside our bodies, or **internal**. They all fit together to make up our skeletons. Other animals have internal skeletons as well.

● Look at these bones from other animals. Which bones do the same job as ours? Name some of the bones.

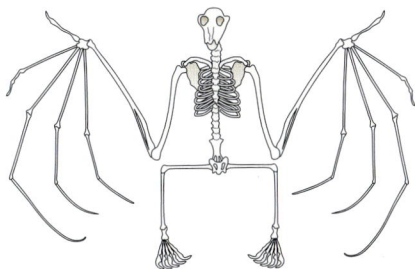

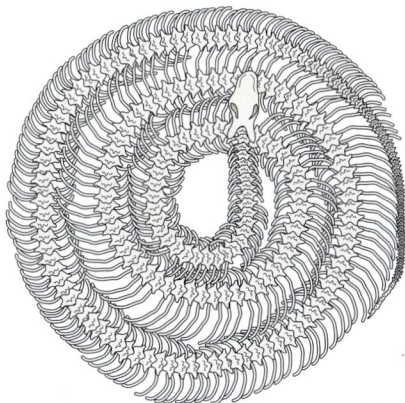

These are the skeletons of a bat and a snake

I wonder…

Watch a dog walking. How can you recognize some of the bones it has? Why can't you see them?

Dig deeper

Find out:
● more about other animals' bones
● why we have bone **marrow** in the centre of our bones.

Did you know?

● There are about 206 bones in your body. Over half of them are in your hands and feet! Each hand has 27 bones and each foot has 26.
● Babies are born with nearly 300 bones. By the time they are an adult, they have only about 206. This is because some bones fuse or bond together. The collar-bone is the last to fuse, when we are about 20 years old.

Broken bones

Things to learn

- Descriptions of the appearance and feel of bones.
- Names of some important bones in the body.
- Bones need to be strong, but can break.

A dog's dinner

Dogs chew the bones of other animals. The bones have a soft, tasty **core** called bone marrow. Chicken bones are brittle and **splinter** easily. They can hurt the insides of a dog's throat.

Bones are strong

Our bones are made from a material containing calcium. Calcium is also in teeth – and in eggshells! Bones are very strong. But they snap if you give them a sudden hard knock. Then they break, like an eggshell. You can move because of joints between your bones. Some joints are like hinges.

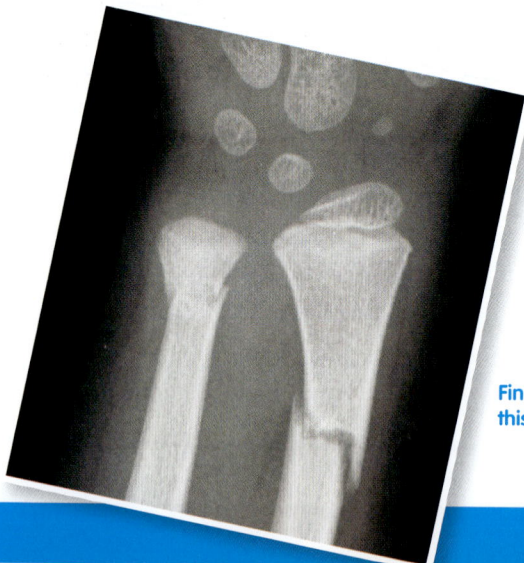

The elbow joint moves like a hinge

humerus

raduis

ulna

Find the break in this arm bone

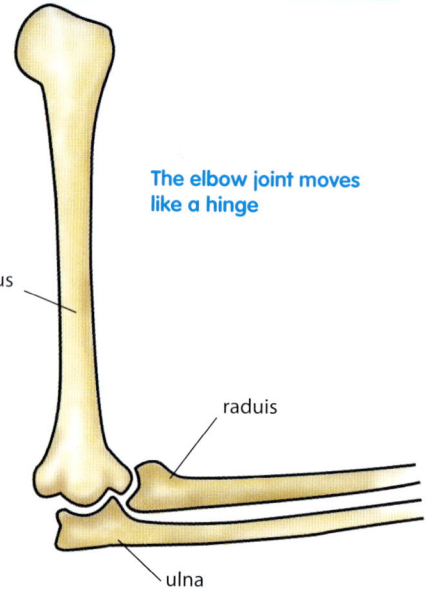

From outer space

X-rays were discovered over 100 years ago, by Wilhelm Röntgen. He first used them to look through his wife's hand. He could see her bones. X-rays pass through your flesh, but are stopped by your bones.

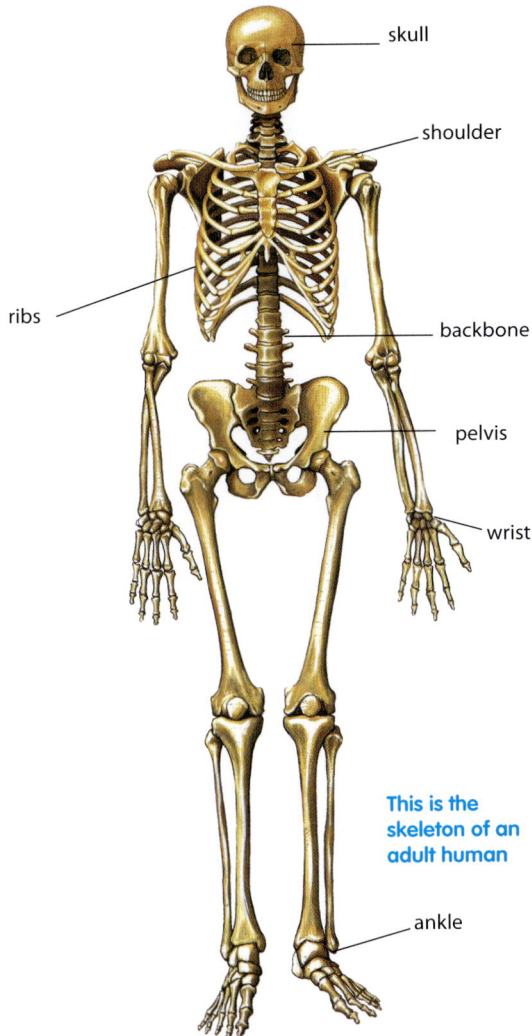

skull

shoulder

ribs

backbone

pelvis

wrist

This is the skeleton of an adult human

ankle

I wonder...

Which is the bone that people break most often — and why?

Dig deeper

Find out:
- more about how bones break
- how bones mend themselves.

Did you know?

- Young chickens have a soft breastbone. It hardens with calcium as the chicken gets older. Inside a young chicken, you can see the soft, **flexible** breastbone.
- Your **knuckles** crack because pulling on them quickly makes a **vacuum** in the joints. Fluid rushes into the spaces, making a popping sound.

Things to do

Looking at bones

- How many bones can you name? Your **ribs**, **skull**, or **backbone**? Label them on a diagram of the skeleton.
- Name all the bones you can.

Growing bones

Your challenge

- Find out if our skeletons grow when we do.
- Measure lengths accurately.
- Decide if the evidence supports your ideas.

Are all our bones the same size?

Our bones are all different lengths. Think of your finger and your leg.

But why is my mother taller than me?

As we grow our bones grow as well. Let's measure some to prove it.

What to do

Class 4 want to see if bones get bigger as we grow. They have decided to measure bones on themselves, some students from Class 3 and Class 5, their teacher and their teaching assistant. They are not sure how much evidence to collect. Here are some of their suggestions.

Which do you think is best?

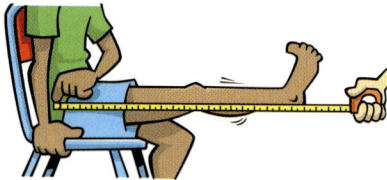

We could measure the legs of the students and the arms of the adults.

We could measure every forearm.

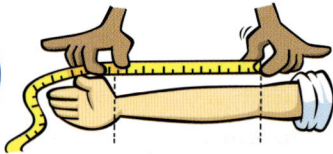

We could get everyone to stand in a line and look at their arm lengths.

What you need

- Rulers or tape measures.

What to check

Now try it yourselves.

- What are you going to measure?
- What will you keep the same to make it a fair test?
- Who will have the biggest bones? Can you explain why?

What did you find?

The students in Class 4 decided to measure the **forearms** of everyone they could. Here are some of their measurements.

Name	Length of forearm (cm)
Anya (age 7)	13
Deven (age 8)	15
Nisha (age 9)	18
Miss Shah	23
Mr Patel	25

- What kind of chart can you produce of Class 4's results? Try it by hand. Then use a computer to draw it.
- What does your chart show? Which person had the longest bones? Why do you think that was? Does this support the idea that bones get bigger as we grow?

- How easy is your chart to understand? Take it to another class. Can they work out what your chart shows?

Can you do better?

- Did you measure accurately?
- How would you change the way you collected your evidence?
- Are there any other questions you could ask?

Now predict

Class 4E are also trying to find out if your bones grow when you get older. They have decided just to measure the forearms of their classmates.

- What is wrong with their idea? How would you show them a better way to collect the evidence?
- Class 4W have decided to measure the leg bones and forearms of their classmates. Can you predict what they will find out? How will their evidence be different from Class 4E's?

Things to learn

- Your skeleton supports your body.
- Some animals have other ways of supporting their bodies.
- Your skeleton protects the inside of your body.

Jellyfish in the sea

Have you ever wondered what we would look like without a skeleton? Just look at a jellyfish on the beach.

Sea water supports a jellyfish's body. It doesn't have a skeleton. When it isn't in the sea, the jellyfish collapses.

Go to bed early, grow very tall...

'Go to bed early, grow very tall, go to bed late, stay very small', or so they say!

When you go to bed, your backbone relaxes. The spongy discs in between the bones of your back relax. They are less squashed. When you get up in the morning, you are very slightly taller than when you went to bed! Try measuring yourself very accurately. Is it true?

Lose weight!

Space does funny things to people! When astronauts go into space they don't experience gravity. Their bones don't have to support their weight. Their bones start to get thinner and lighter. Astronauts weigh less when they come back to Earth than when they took off.

Things to do

Totally spineless

Worms, snails and slugs don't have a skeleton inside their body. How do they keep their shape?

● Look at a crab or large insect. They have a skeleton on the outside of their body. How do you think they support themselves?

How strong?

Bones are very strong. They are also hollow. They contain a jelly-like substance called marrow. Hollow bones are strong but light enough to move.

● Roll sheets of paper to create different shaped towers. Glue or tape them into rolls. Place some books or weights on the top of the towers. Which one holds the most? How strong are hollow shapes?

I wonder…

If you put a tooth in cola or vinegar it will decay. What do you think might happen to a bone in cola or vinegar? Explain why.

Dig deeper

Find out:
● more about your skeleton
● another word for 'backbone'
● what three jobs a skeleton does.

Did you know?

● We have tiny bones at the end of our backbones that were once tails! We also have some muscles that should **wiggle** our ears! Not everyone can do this.
● The garfish has green bones!
● Some snakes can digest bones and teeth.

Contracting muscles

Things to learn

- Our skeletons have muscles attached to them.
- Muscles contract to make bones move.
- Muscles work in pairs.

A nose like an elephant's

An elephant has a strong flexible nose. It has over 40 000 **muscles** in it! All these muscles mean the elephant can pick up a **delicate** flower or lift a huge log. The trunk can also touch, grasp, suck, spray, smell and strike!

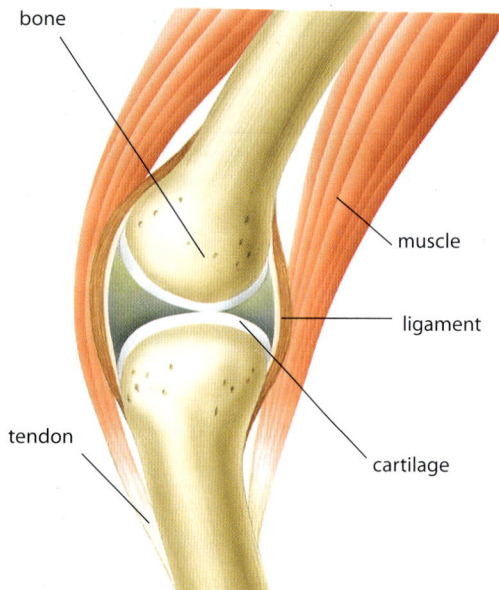

bone

muscle

ligament

tendon

cartilage

This is a hinge joint, which you find in your elbows, knees, fingers and toes

Our muscles are our motors

Your skeleton gives **protection** and support. The muscles are the motors of your body. Muscles are connected to your bones by **tendons**. A joint is where two bones meet, like your elbow or shoulder.

When the muscle **contracts** it pulls on the tendon. This pulls on the bone to make it move. Muscles can pull (contract). They cannot push, only **relax**. We need two muscles at each joint. One pulls in one direction and the other pulls in the opposite direction. As one pulls, the other relaxes. They work in pairs.

Things to do

Contract and relax?

When you move your forearm up and down at the elbow, two sets of muscles are working.

● Put your hand on your upper arm. Can you feel which muscles contract when you lift your forearm? What happens to the muscles under your arm?

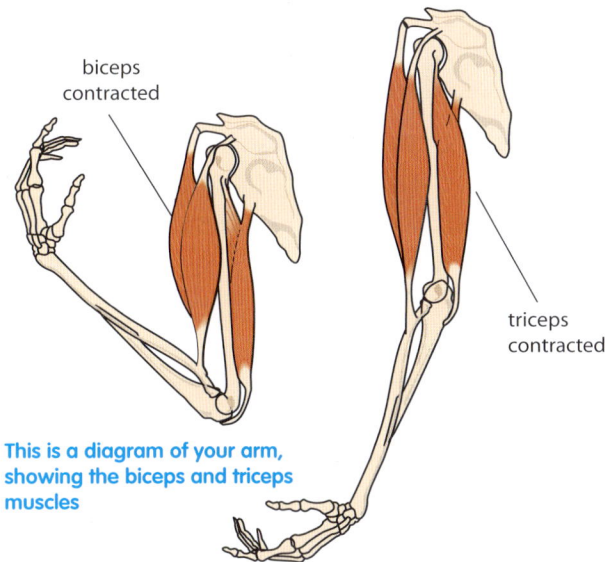

biceps contracted

triceps contracted

This is a diagram of your arm, showing the biceps and triceps muscles

Where are there other pairs of muscles in your body?

I wonder...

Watch someone smile and frown. Can you see the muscles contract?

Caterpillars

● Watch a caterpillar moving across some paper. It has over 2000 muscles in its body. We have only 600. Does a caterpillar have a skeleton? Describe how a caterpillar moves. How do the muscles contract and relax?

Dig deeper

Find out:
● more about muscles
● the names of different types of muscles.

Did you know?

● You need 72 muscles to speak a single word!
● It takes 17 facial muscles to smile, but 42 to frown. So smiling is easier!
● The hairs on your body help to trap heat. Each hair is attached to a tiny muscle. It makes the hair stand on end when you are cold! Some people call this muscle contraction 'goose pimples' or 'goose skin'.

Things to learn

- Muscles work harder when we exercise.
- We feel tired when muscles work hard.

Tireless muscle

Our muscles work every time we move. Do all of them work at the same time? Your heart works all the time, even if you don't tell it to! It beats about 100 000 times each day. If you had to tell it to work, your heart would stop when you went to sleep. What would happen then?

Your intestines pass food along inside your body. They work all the time. Do you have to tell them to work? Many parts of your body work without you thinking. Which muscles only work when you think about them?

Muscles can grow

Have you watched competitions to find the strongest man or woman? These people have much bigger muscles than us. How do they develop them? Was it easy to develop these muscles?

Try the activity on the next page. Discover what happens when you exercise. How does exercise help keep you fit?

Things to do

Exercise

- Sit very still and quiet! Think about how you feel. Close your eyes and pay attention to your body. Now get up and walk around the room. After a couple of minutes, stop. How is your body different?
- Now stand behind your chair. Put your hands on the top of the chair. Start moving up and down. Stop as soon as you feel different. Explain the changes to your body. Why do these changes happen?

Exercise keeps you fit

I wonder...

If you exercise regularly, your muscles become less tired when you exercise. Why do you think this is?

Dig deeper

Find out:
- about muscles in hands and feet
- what is so special about our fingers and thumbs.

Did you know?

- A cat has over 30 muscles in each earflap. We have only 6!
- Walking uses 200 muscles in the human body. It takes 40 muscles to lift the leg and move it forward.
- Your heart is a hollow muscle about the same size as your fist. It pumps 36 000 litres of blood 12 000 miles every day!

Drugs as medicine

Things to learn

- A **drug** is a substance that affects the way our body works.
- Medicines are types of drugs.
- Different medicines can be given in different ways to make you feel better.

Drugs to help us

A **drug** is any substance which changes the way our body works. We take **medicines** when we are ill. Medicines are drugs to make us feel better. We must take medicines at the right time and take the right amounts. We must not give them to other people.

Getting better

Some medicines we take for a very short time. Others we take for several days, weeks or even years. What different ways have you taken medicines? Did the medicine make you better?

Taking medicine

We take medicines in lots of different ways. Sometimes we swallow them, like tablets or liquids. They are absorbed through our stomach. Sometimes we have medicine injected into us. Other medicines work best when we **inhale** them or rub them onto our body.

Things to do

Staying safe

Look at the way medicines are packaged. Why is medicine packaging special?

I wonder...

Some people say 'prevention is better than cure'. What do they mean?

Dig deeper

Find out:
- how to **dispose** of medicines when you have finished with them
- about natural **remedies** used to **prevent** or treat illness.

Did you know?

- The Ancient Greeks, Romans and people in medieval Europe all had medicinal gardens. They grew plants in them to use as medicine.
- Bark from the willow tree has some of the same ingredients as modern aspirin.
- Quinine is a drug for treating malaria and fever. It was first used by the Indians of South America. They found it in the bark of cinchona trees.

What have you learned?

- Some animals have internal skeletons like humans.
- Bones are very strong, but they can break.
- Our skeletons grow bigger as we grow up.
- Our skeletons support and protect our bodies and help us to move.
- Muscles contract or shorten to make bones move.
- We have muscles that work in pairs to help us move.
- Medicines are taken in different ways to make us feel better.

Find out more about...

- how bones grow and develop in babies
- what Eadweard Muybridge discovered about how animals move.

Check-up

Class 4W were having a PE lesson. They were running on the spot and felt tired.

- Print out a picture of the human skeleton and muscles. Draw arrows to those bones and muscles Class 4W used most when running.
- Explain why they felt tired after exercise.

The answer!

Do you remember the question about **recovering** after a broken bone?

If you break your leg, the doctor puts a **plaster cast** on it. This keeps it still and straight. As you are not using the muscles of that leg, they become weak. The leg becomes thin. You need to do some gentle exercise to build the muscles back up again.

Unit 2: Living things in their environment

Would a dolphin survive in a wood? What about in a pond? Would a large tree grow big and strong in a pond? Every living thing, plant or animal has its own special place to live that suits it best. This is called its habitat.

What do you know?

- Plants and animals are living things.
- Animals need food to grow and be healthy.
- Plants need light, warmth, air and water to grow well.
- Plants grow towards the Sun.

Words to learn

adaptation
classification
condition
consumer
environment
food chain
habitat
key
nutrition
organism
pollution
predator
prey
producer
variation
wild

Skills check

Can you...

- measure time, distance and temperature?
- make careful observations?
- explain what you found out through science?

Let's find out...

In some countries some people want to protect the countryside. When they travel through it, they take care not to damage it. They plant **wild** flowers in their gardens. They leave logs lying around. This can look very untidy. So why do they do these things?

Different habitats

Things to learn

- A habitat is a place where plants and animals live naturally.
- Different animals and plants live in different habitats.
- Plants and animals survive best in their own habitat.

Where should we live?

We find camels in the deserts. We also find humans! We find polar bears in the Arctic. We also find humans! Humans can live almost anywhere in the world! Unlike other animals, we wear clothes and live in houses to survive.

Camels live in the desert

In the desert, people wear long, light, **flowing** robes. They wear clothes to protect skin from the Sun. They may build large houses of stone to keep cool.

In the Arctic people wear thick furs to keep warm. They wear boots on their feet and gloves on their hands. They build houses that help to keep them warm. Plants and animals can't do that.

Are you in the habit?

Where do you go when your school day is over? You probably go home. It's a **habit**. It is a habit to return to your home or habitat.

A **habitat** is a place where an animal or plant lives. It is a place that provides food and **shelter**. A habitat is a place where living things produce **offspring**.

Penguins live in the Antarctic

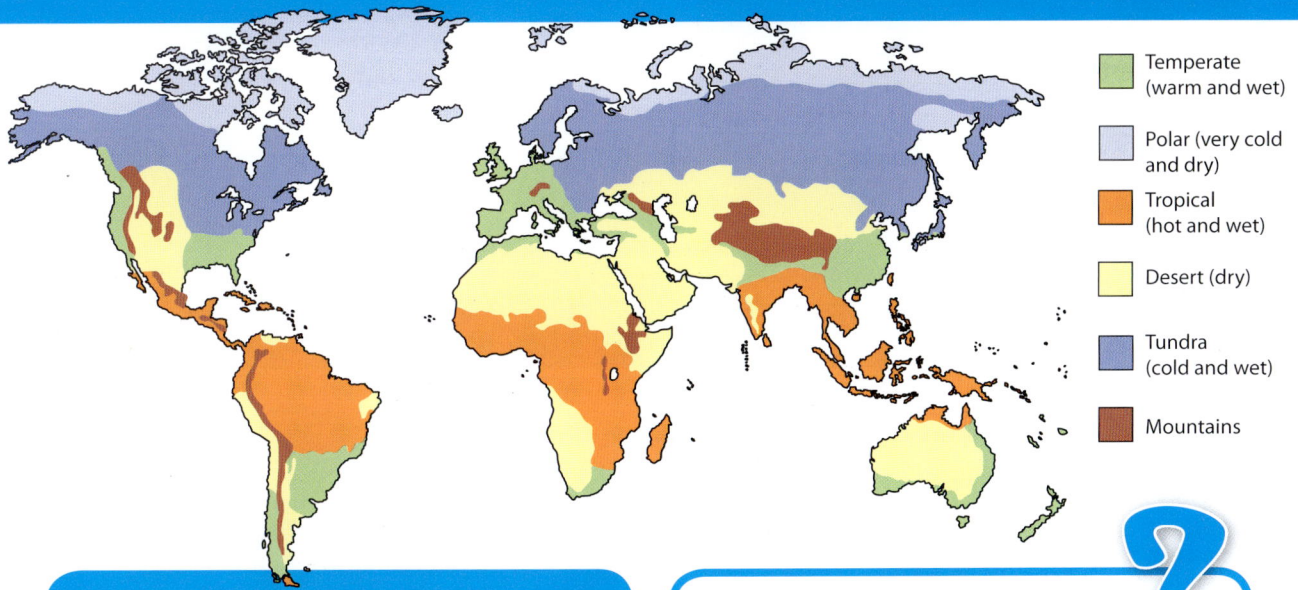

	Temperate (warm and wet)
	Polar (very cold and dry)
	Tropical (hot and wet)
	Desert (dry)
	Tundra (cold and wet)
	Mountains

Things to do

Let's investigate habitats

Walk around your school.

- Can you recognize any different habitats? Look at how different they are. What differences are there?
- How many habitats can you describe around the school?

Where do you live?

- Where can a snail live? Where does a scorpion or a snake live?
- What lives in your habitat? Why do these plants and animals live there?
- Which animals like dark, damp habitats under logs or beneath stones?

Dig deeper

Find out:
- more about what a habitat is
- why a camel can't survive where a polar bear lives.

Did you know?

- The oceans are up to seven miles deep. They cover over 70% of the world. Animals in the deep-sea habitat are **adapted** to living in the dark.
- Camels have long eyelashes to protect their eyes from blowing sand. They are adapted to life in the desert.

I wonder...

It's cool and wet. The plants float. The animals swim. Can you guess what the habitat is? What animals would you expect to find here?

Grouping living things

Things to learn

- There are similarities and differences between animals.
- Animals can be grouped by their similarities.
- Plants can also be grouped by their similarities.

How are they different?

It's easy to spot differences between animals. Lions are big; mice are small. But they are similar. Both have fur, four legs and a tail. Lizards are small and they have four legs and a tail. But they have no fur. Mice are more like lions than like lizards!

Even a skunk is a mammal!

The same but different

All animals take in **oxygen**, feed, grow, reproduce, and more. But are all animals the same? Is a cat like a fish? Or a frog like a bird? Scientists have sorted animals into groups. We are in a group called **mammals**. Mammals have a backbone, are warm-blooded and have fur or hair. They have live babies and feed them milk. Dogs, cats, whales and camels are also mammals. This means we are all in the same group. Are we like them?

Plants are also sorted into groups. Some are trees, some are **shrubs** and some are grasses.

Carolus Linnaeus devised the groups of plants and animals we use today

I wonder...

Why is a whale a mammal and not a fish?

Dig deeper

Find out:
- more about how living things are classified
- what language is used for the scientific names of plants and animals.

Things to do

What are you like?

Over 250 years ago a scientist called Carolus Linnaeus sorted living things into groups. This is called **classification**.

- Can you sort your own selection of plants and animals into groups? Explain how you have grouped them. Explain why you put them into these groups. Some reasons could be colour, shape, wings or number of legs. Can you think of more?

Did you know?

- Nearly one quarter of all mammals are bats!
- One large group of animals contains dogs, bears and cats – including big cats like the lion. Dogs, foxes and wolves all belong to the same, smaller group.
- When people first saw a giraffe, they called it a 'cameleopard'. They thought its parents were a camel and a leopard!

Using keys

Things to learn

- Animals and plants can be identified by their features.
- We can identify them with keys.

Unlocking

Keys unlock things – they let you enter where you want to go. You use a key to get into your house. You even use a key – a password – on your computer. A key is used to identify different animals and plants. It 'unlocks' their **identity**.

What's my name

Use Key 1 and Key 2. Find out the name of the boy in this photo. Which key is easier to use? Why?

Key 1

Q1
I am a boy	Go to Q2
I am a girl	Go to Q4

Q2
I have black hair	Go to Q3
I have fair hair	I am Richi

Q3
I live in UAE	I am Ismael
I live in India	I am Anwar

Q4
I have long hair	I am Yasmin
I have short hair	I am Hannah

Key 2

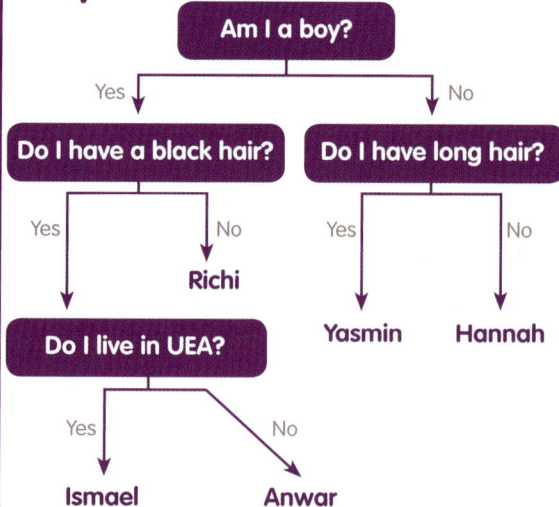

Things to do

What am I?

Can you identify a range of animals and plants? Go to one of your habitats. Carefully collect some animals. Remember where you got them from, so you can return them later. Use some keys, like the ones on page 22, to identify them. Can you make your own key? Ask simple questions that have 'yes' or 'no' answers. Try writing a key in both styles.

Dig deeper

Find out:
- more about evolution and Charles Darwin.
- where he travelled to and what he found.

Evolution is the process that has changed animals and plants over millions of years. It explains why plants and animals are found in different groups.

I wonder...

Make up an animal. Name it so that everyone can identify it. Think carefully about how it looks. Use your description to give it a name.

Did you know?

- Tomatoes are in the same plant group as tobacco.
- The banana and a beautiful plant called 'the bird of paradise' are from the same family of plants!
- The giant seaweeds that make up underwater forests are in the same group as pond weeds, which are usually tiny!

Investigating invertebrates

Your challenge

- Investigate what conditions invertebrates like to live in.
- Make a reliable observation.
- Explain your evidence scientifically.

I wonder what other kinds of invertebrates we could investigate here?

Worms?

Spiders?

Ants?

Beetles?

How could we find out what conditions they like?

What to do

Mrs Choudry was talking to her grandson in Germany on the Internet.

At school we've been looking at invertebrates, Gran.

What have you found out?

We've been finding out where they like to live. They like dark and damp places.

Class 4 counted the worms before they put them in. They had 30 worms. Why did they do this? Would you use any of their ideas?

What you need

- A digital camera or a video camera with a timer
- A fish tank
- Leaves, stones, twigs, soil, moss, compost, bark, sand.

Back in school Mrs Choudry told her class what her grandson had been investigating. Class 4 discussed what invertebrates they might find around their school. They decided to look at worms. They set up a fish tank with lots of different areas. They put the worms in the tank. They agreed to leave the tank alone for a day to see what happened.

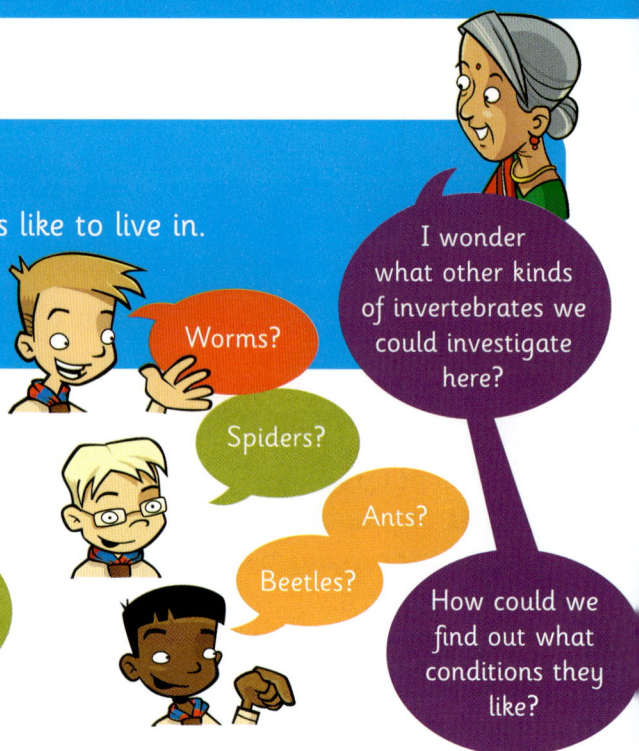

What to check

Now try it yourselves.

- What information are you going to collect?
- What do you think will happen?

I think that we should count the worms after a day to see if they are all still there.

Our group thinks that you should count the worms in each area after one day.

We could take photographs of where the worms are at the start and then after a day.

We could use the video camera to film the worms for a day.

- Draw a table of your results or use Class 4's results. Use a computer to record your results and draw a chart. What kind of chart or graph do you think would be best?
- What does your chart show? Which habitat did the worms like best?

Can you do better?

What would you do differently if you tried this again? Would using more invertebrates improve the investigation? What about different habitats?

What did you find?

Class 4 drew a table of their results after a day.

Habitat in tank	Number of worms
leaves	4
wet soil	20
dry soil	5
bark	0
stones	0
twigs	1

Now predict

- Class 3 are going out to collect worms so they can draw them. Where would you tell them to look for worms?
- Class 5 don't want to collect worms. They have decided to look for **centipedes**. Where do you think you would find a centipede? Why?
- Why was it better to use lots of worms rather than just a few?

Food chains

Things to learn

- Some animals eat other animals in their habitat.
- A food chain shows who eats who, or what, in a habitat.

Where does energy come from?

All animals eat to give them energy. They need energy to grow and live. Where does that energy come from?

A seal gets its energy from eating other animals. It eats fish or penguins.

The penguins get their energy from eating fish.

The fish get their energy from eating tiny green plants called plankton.

The plankton get their energy from the Sun.

This brown bear looks hungry

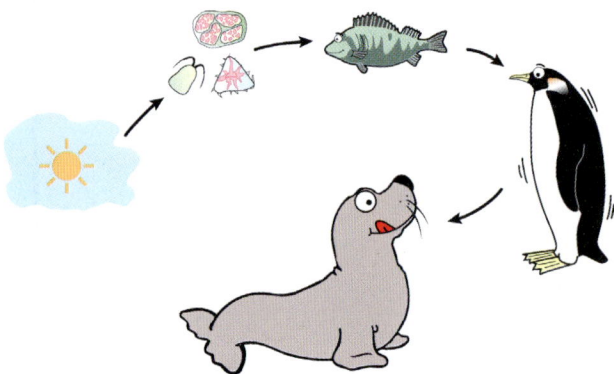

A saltwater food chain

Predator and prey

An animal that eats another animal is called a **predator**. The animal it eats is called its **prey**. Can you spot the predators and prey in the **food chains** on page 27? A predator may also be the prey of another animal!

A green plant is called a **producer** because it produces the food for animals. How does the Sun help it to produce this food? Which are the producers in these food chains?

Things to do

Short and simple

- Draw a food chain. The arrows show the direction that the energy is flowing.
- Look at some of the habitats around your school. Draw a food chain for each one. You will need to find what each **organism** eats. What does each food chain start with?
- Produce a food chain for an animal in the zoo, like a bear or a snake.

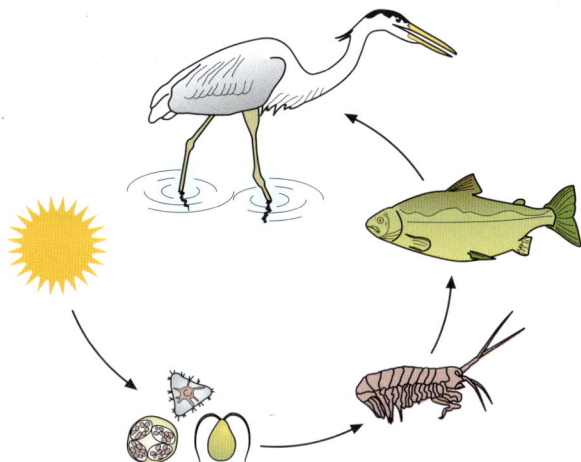

A freshwater food chain

Dig deeper

Find out:
- more about how food chains work
- what a food web is.

I wonder...

Where does all food energy originally come from? Where do the plants get their energy from?

A tropical food chain

Did you know?

- A shark is an efficient predator. It can smell one drop of blood in 450 million litres of sea water! It can smell blood from over ten miles away.
- The blue whale is the largest animal on Earth. It lives on some of the smallest animals – **krill** and small shrimps.
- A humpback whale eats 5000 fish a day. The fish will have eaten 7000 **shrimps**. The shrimps will have eaten 130 000 tiny green plants. It takes four billion green plants to feed a humpback whale every day!

Things to learn
- Animals are adapted to their habitat.
- Living things and their habitats need protecting.

All change

Imagine a house cat catching and killing elephants. Imagine keeping a tiger in your sitting room. Not very practical is it? But they are both cats. How are they different?

Each is adapted to suit where it lives. The tiger has large claws and jaws for catching its prey. House cats have smaller claws and jaws.

The tiger is a member of the cat family

Do you want to visit my place?

Some animals are adapted to living in water. Some are adapted to living on land. Some animals can live in both habitats. We call them amphibians.

A frog is adapted to living in the habitats of both the oryx and the fish. Can you explain why? Name some other amphibians that are adapted to living in two different habitats?

Things to do

Save our habitat

- Walk around your school playground. Look at the habitats. Have they changed since you looked at them last? What would happen if someone built a house on the playing field? Or filled in a pond? Think about the animals and the plants that live there.

- Fungi like these grow in damp places. Fungi are not plants. They grow on rotting plant materials. Some are very beautiful. But their habitat can be dark and damp. Sometimes we need to keep dark, damp places.

I wonder...

What can you do to protect the environment in your area?

Dig deeper

Find out:
- more about protecting the environment
- what is damaging our environment.

Did you know?

- Recycling a pile of newspapers 1.5 metres high could save a 15-metre high tree from being pulped to make paper.
- A plastic container could take as long as 50 000 years to rot away!

Our environment

Things to learn

● Recognize ways that human activity affects the environment.

Problem pollution

Pollution is spoiling a natural area. Humans are often responsible for spoiling natural areas. People may dump waste from industry or manufacturing. They may introduce polluting materials like oil into the environment.

Dirty water

Clean water is one of the Earth's most valuable natural resources. Without it there would be no life. When we put **waste products** in the sea, we endanger plants and animals living in or near the water.

This sea bird has been coated with crude oil

Smoke from industry can pollute the air

Cleaning up

Plastic bags, old tyres, bottles and cans can pollute the sea. We can remove these from water fairly easily. Other **pollutants** can't be seen. They dissolve and so are more difficult to get out. **Sewage** and **fertilizers** from farms can pollute clean water.

In some countries bins are used to collect waste for recycling

I wonder...

What can I do today to cut down on waste?

Things to do

Reduce, re-use, recycle

In the natural world there's no such thing as waste. Everything that living things produce is broken down and re-used. Each year each one of us produces about ¾ of a tonne of household waste. All of that rubbish has to go somewhere! Many of the things we throw away could be re-used or recycled. Some we really don't need at all!

Look around your classroom. Make a list of things that could be used again or recycled. How many things can you find that are used once before they are thrown away?

Dig deeper

Find out:
- what household waste in your area is re-used or recycled
- what you can do to be more **energy efficient**
- about **renewable energy**.

Did you know?

- The average person in America uses nearly 2 million litres of water a year.
- Glass can be recycled over and over again. It never decays.

Unit 2: Review

What have you learned?

- Different animals and plants are found in different habitats.
- Plants and animals can be grouped by features they have in common.
- How to create and use a key to identify some animals and plants.
- Animals and plants are adapted to their environment.
- We need to protect the habitats that animals and plants live in.

Find out more about...

- how some animals change to suit their environment
- how changing the habitat affects the animals and plants living there.

Check-up

Class 4 are going for a picnic. They need to treat their environment carefully. They must not **disturb** the animals and plants living there.

- Explain why they should not damage habitats.
- Explain why they mustn't break food chains.
- Explain why there will be more plants and animals if we care for habitats.

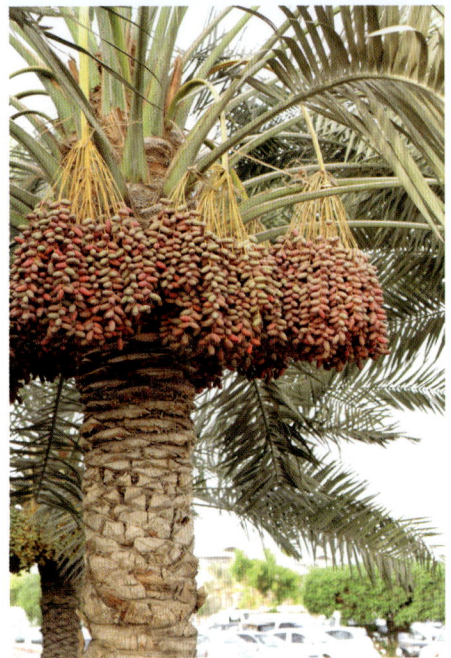

A date palm can produce many kilos of dates, which feed many animals

The answer!

Remember the first question? Wild flowers provide bees and other insects with a source of food. Logs are places for small animals like beetles to live. Not being too tidy in the garden helps wildlife to survive. It gives them shelter and food. It provides their habitat.

Unit 3: Keeping warm

What do you wear to go to the beach? How does the sea feel after you've been playing in the Sun? Do you want hot soup or ice cream? What happens to ice cream if you don't eat it fast enough? Would it happen if you kept the ice cream in a freezer?

What do you know?

- Materials have many different properties.
- Some materials have similar properties.
- Some properties are useful to us.
- Some materials are good conductors of heat and some are good insulators.

Skills check

Can you...
- read a ruler accurately?
- use a computer for your work?

Words to learn

Celsius	insulation
conduct	temperature
degrees	thermal
heat	thermometer
insulate	

Let's find out...

Not all countries are hot. In cold countries, the **loft** can be the hottest part of the house. That's because heat rises. Heat can escape through the roof and the house will get cold. A layer of soft, **fluffy** material is put in the loft to keep the house warm. This material is called loft **insulation**. What would be a good material to slow down the escape of heat? Will a house in a cold country get warm if there is no heating?

Feeling hot

Things to learn

- Temperature is a measure of how hot or cold things are.
- A thermometer measures temperature.
- Our senses are not accurate thermometers.

Sense of…

How many senses do you have? Where are they found in your body? You have at least five senses – touch, taste, sight, hearing and smell. You have eyes, ears, a nose and a mouth. The sense of touch is found all over your body. What do you use for sensing **heat**? Can you smell heat or see it? Can you hear it?

Which sense do you use to tell the flame is hot?

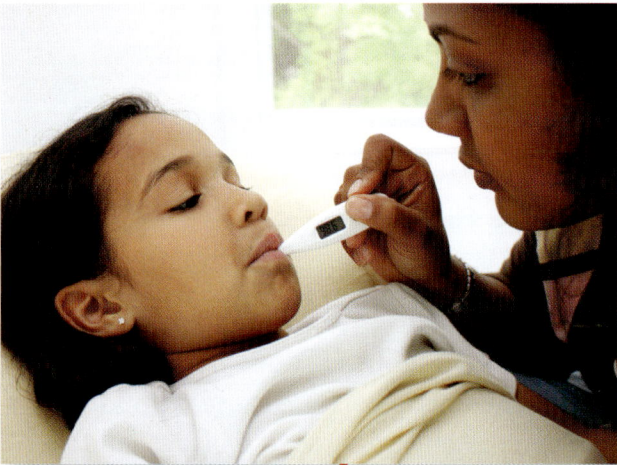

What temperature should the thermometer read if the child is well?

Feeling hot

When you are ill, an adult may feel your forehead. They may say you 'have a **temperature**'. They mean that you are warmer than usual. A high temperature may mean you are not well. But touching your forehead does not give an accurate temperature reading. A **thermometer** can measure how hot you are. Normally your body temperature should be 37°C. This means that on a thermometer with a **Celsius** scale, your temperature reads 37°. Some thermometers have a Fahrenheit (F) scale. Your temperature should be 98.4°F.

Things to do

Heat sense

How do you know if something is hot? If it is safe, you may feel it. You use your sense of touch. Is this good enough?

- Put one hand in a bowl of hot tap water. Put the other in a bowl of cold iced water. Keep them there for two minutes.
- Then put both hands into a bowl of water at room temperature.
- Describe what you feel.

I wonder...

Thermometers are filled with a liquid dye. They look red, green or blue. Some older thermometers are filled with **mercury**. Why is this no longer used?

Dig deeper

Find out:
- about different kinds of thermometers
- if medical thermometers that change colour with temperature are accurate.

Did you know?

- The first thermometer was invented 500 years ago by the **astronomer** Galileo Galilei.
- The first medical thermometer was made in 1867.
- Thermometers work because the liquid in them **expands** or contracts until it is the same temperature as the surroundings. This can be measured on a temperature scale.

Measuring temperature

Things to learn

- A thermometer measures temperature.
- There are lots of different thermometers.
- Thermometers must be handled with care.
- Objects gain or lose heat until they reach room temperature.

How hot?

A thermometer is used to measure how hot or cold something is. A thermometer has a liquid in it that expands when the temperature gets hotter. If the liquid in the thermometer expands, the object is hot.

What temperatures are these thermometers showing? Which shows the highest temperature?

Different thermometers record temperatures in different places. Some are used outside, some in science and some for people. Where do you think we would use these thermometers?

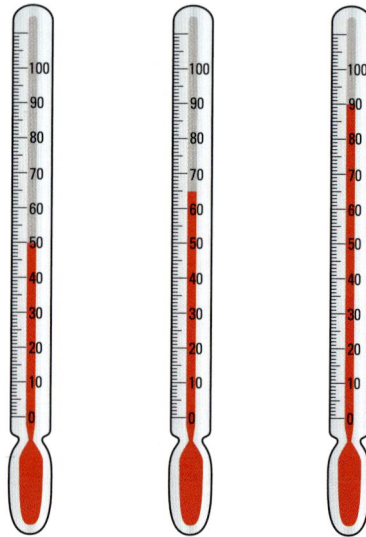

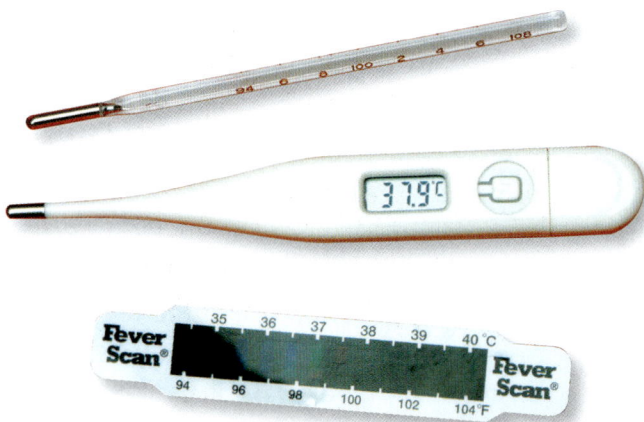

Room temperature

Neema put her meal on the table – hot soup and vanilla ice cream. Then the telephone rang. She went to answer it. She was a long time on the phone. When she got back, the soup was cold and the ice cream had melted. The soup had lost heat. The ice cream had gained heat. The soup and the ice cream were both at room temperature.

I wonder…

If you put beakers of water at different temperatures in a fridge, what final temperature would they all have?

Things to do

Final temperature

What temperature is your classroom? Use a thermometer to find out.

- Place five marked beakers in a row. Half fill each one with water from different places, like the fridge or the hot or cold tap. Take the starting temperature of the water in each beaker. Write it down. Then take it again an hour later.
- Use the thermometer properly. Keep the bulb of the thermometer in the water. Bend down so that your eye is level with the thermometer. Keep the thermometer upright. Don't stir the liquid with the thermometer. What will happen if you leave the water and take its temperature after one day? What has happened? Why? What pattern or rule is there about temperatures over time?

Biographies

Find out:
- more about the first modern thermometer made by Gabriel Daniel Fahrenheit.

Did you know?

- America is the only country still using Fahrenheit scale for measuring temperature. All other countries use the Celsius scale.
- There are several different scales for measuring temperature. They include Fahrenheit, Kelvin, Celsius, Reaumur and Rankine!

Hot and cold places

Things to learn

- Different places are at different temperatures.
- 20°C is a comfortable room temperature.

Hot or not?

Have you ever been abroad on holiday? Do you know someone who has? Would you prefer a hot or a cold place? If you listen to weather reports, they tell you the temperature for the next day. What pattern do you notice about the temperatures? If you wanted to be cool, where on this map would you go?

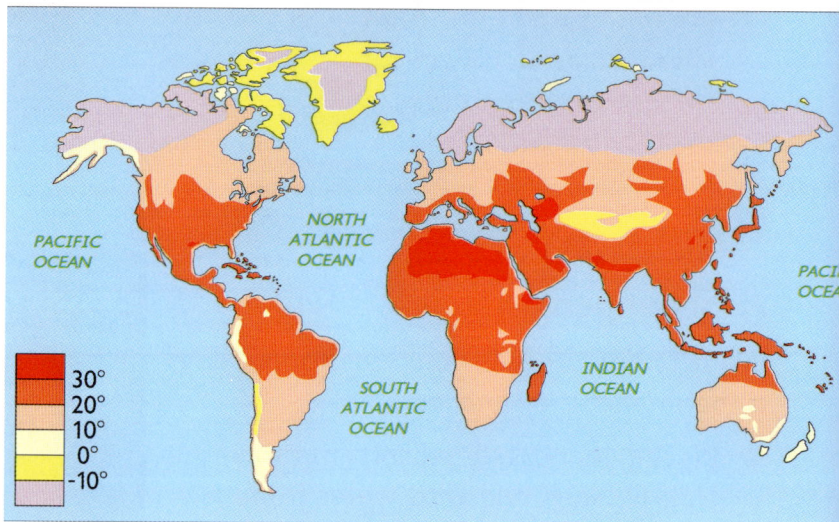

PACIFIC OCEAN

NORTH ATLANTIC OCEAN

PACIFIC OCEAN

SOUTH ATLANTIC OCEAN

INDIAN OCEAN

30°
20°
10°
0°
-10°

World map showing average temperatures

window sill

fridge

Keeping your cool

Look at this plan of a kitchen. Where would you put some seedlings to grow well? Where would you keep your can of fizzy drink so that it stays cool? Would this be a hot or a cold place? What helped you to decide?

Are all the places in this kitchen the same temperature? If you had an **ice lolly** where would you keep it? What would happen if you didn't?

Things to do

Hot spots

- Draw a plan of your classroom including air-conditioning units, fans and radiators. If you were cold, where would you want to sit? Why? If you were too hot you might want to sit in a different place. Is there any scientific reason for this?
- Put a blue cross on your plan where you think it will be cool. Put a red cross where you think it is warmer. How could you discover if you are right?
- Plan your investigation carefully. Choose the place and the type of thermometer. Mark red and blue circles to show your results on your plan.
- Why is it warmer in some places than in others?

This food container keeps food cool

I wonder...

Will another classroom be a different temperature? Where will the hot and cool spots be? Why?

Dig deeper

Find out:
- which materials conduct heat. We call these good thermal **conductors**
- examples of poor thermal conductors.

Did you know?

- Homes in cold countries need heating to keep them warm. 20°C is a comfortable room temperature.
- Homes in warm countries use air-conditioning to keep cool. It keeps temperatures close to 20°C in the summer.

Keeping cool

- Use a thermometer carefully and accurately.
- Investigate the best way to keep ice lollies cold.
- Explain what you found out.
- Communicate your conclusions to others.

I could keep them in the cardboard box they are packed in.

I could take off my socks and put the lollies inside them.

I could put one in my hat to keep the Sun off it.

I could run with them.

I could wrap them, but that might make them warmer.

I could put one in my pocket to shade it from the Sun.

FREEZER

What to do

Farida has got ice lollies for her friends. She has to take the ice lollies to her friends before they **melt**. Will insulation keep the lollies cold? What would you do?

What you need

- A thermometer
- A stopwatch
- Ice lollies
- Pieces of different fabrics.

What to check

Now try it yourselves.

- What will keep the ice lollies cold?
- Why does the starting size of each ice lolly matter?
- How will you measure how well the lollies keep?
- How will you measure the temperature of your ice lollies?

What do you find?

Each lolly was 16 cm long when Farida took it from the freezer.

Farida measured how long her lollies were when she got to her friends. These are her results.

Method of insulation	Length of lolly (cm)
in socks	12
in a hat	13
in cardboard	14
in pocket	11

- Draw a graph of her results.
- Which insulation kept the lollies from melting best? How can you tell?
- What was happening to the lollies?
- Draw a graph of your own results. What sort of graph can you draw? Use a computer to draw your graph as well.
- Which insulation kept the ice lollies frozen longest?

Can you do better?

- Farida measured the length of her lollies to see which melted the most. What other measurement could she have taken?
- Did you use a thermometer? How often did you take the temperature of the ice lollies?

Now predict

- If you wrapped different ice lollies in different thicknesses of newspaper sheets, which lolly would stay frozen longest?
- What is the newspaper doing?

Investigating insulators

Your challenge

- Investigate how to keep liquid hot for a long time.
- Decide what an insulator does.
- Explain what you found out.

DO NOT use boiling water

Class 4 are walking in the mountains where it is very cold. They take tea to warm them up. Hassan has put his tea in a vacuum flask.

Here are some of the ideas the other walkers had to keep their tea warm.

A vacuum flask insulates things – heat can't get in or out easily

a plastic cup with a lid

a metal container with a lid

a plastic cup with a lid, wrapped in a jumper

a metal container with a lid, wrapped in a jumper

a plastic cup with a lid, wrapped in a tissue

a metal container with a lid, wrapped in a tissue

What you need

- Mugs or containers with lids
- Small items of clean clothing
- Thermometers
- A stopwatch
- A measuring jug
- Warm tap water.

What to check

Now try it yourselves.

- Are all your starting temperatures the same?
- Are you keeping all your containers in the same place?

What did you find?

These are the walkers' results:

Container and insulation	Temperature after 40 minutes (°C)
plastic cup with lid	65
metal container with lid	55
plastic cup with lid in a jumper	75
metal container with lid in a jumper	64
plastic cup with lid in a cotton tissue	67
metal container with lid in a cotton tissue	59

Can you do better?

- The walkers used what they would normally carry in their backpacks for their tests.
- What else could you test?
- Was the walkers' test fair? Why?

- Draw a graph of the walkers' results. What type of graph will you draw? Draw one using a computer as well. Which were the best ways of keeping their tea warm?
- From what you found out, which fabric is best at insulating? Look at the fabric carefully. Use a hand lens. What makes a good **thermal** insulator?

Now predict

- Does the starting temperature of the tea matter?
- Air is a good thermal insulator. Trapped air in a woollen jumper is warmed by the tea. A warm 'air overcoat' is wrapped round the tea.
- How could you keep a cold drink cold?

Conducting heat

Things to learn
- Metals are good thermal conductors.
- Good electrical conductors are often good thermal conductors too.
- Thermal insulators are useful.

Hot or cold?

Any material that slows the movement of heat is an insulator. An insulator keeps hot things hot and cold things cold. The same materials will insulate both hot and cold objects. But not both at once!

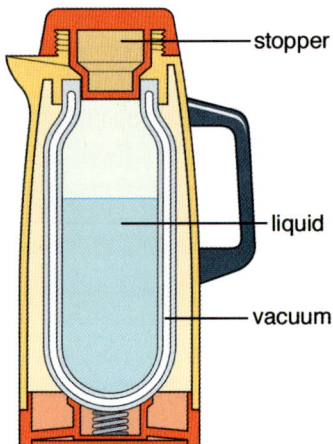

What have you got in your vacuum flask?

Some tea and a choc ice!

Silly boy!

stopper

liquid

vacuum

Vacuum flasks

A vacuum flask is a good insulator. It is like one jug inside another. Between the two jugs there is nothing at all – a vacuum. Heat cannot travel easily through air. It cannot travel at all through a vacuum. Hot food in a vacuum flask stays hot for longer. Cold food stays cold.

Thermal underwear

Thermal means to do with heat. In very cold countries, like Norway and Iceland, people need to wear thermal underwear. What does thermal underwear do? It stops the heat from your body escaping into the air. It keeps you warm. In cold weather you would put on more layers of clothes. The thick fabrics trap air. You warm the air and so you keep warm. But clothes aren't hot themselves. They are at room temperature.

These clothes trap lots of air to keep heat in

Things to do

Runny honey

Find out which materials are good thermal conductors. This means that they **conduct** heat easily.

- Collect spoons of different materials. Smear a small amount of thick honey on the end of each handle. Put the spoons in bowls of hot water and start your stopwatch. Record how long it takes for the honey to go runny on each spoon. On which spoon did the honey melt fastest? Which material conducted the heat fastest?
- Which material would you use to make a saucepan? Which material would you use for the handle?

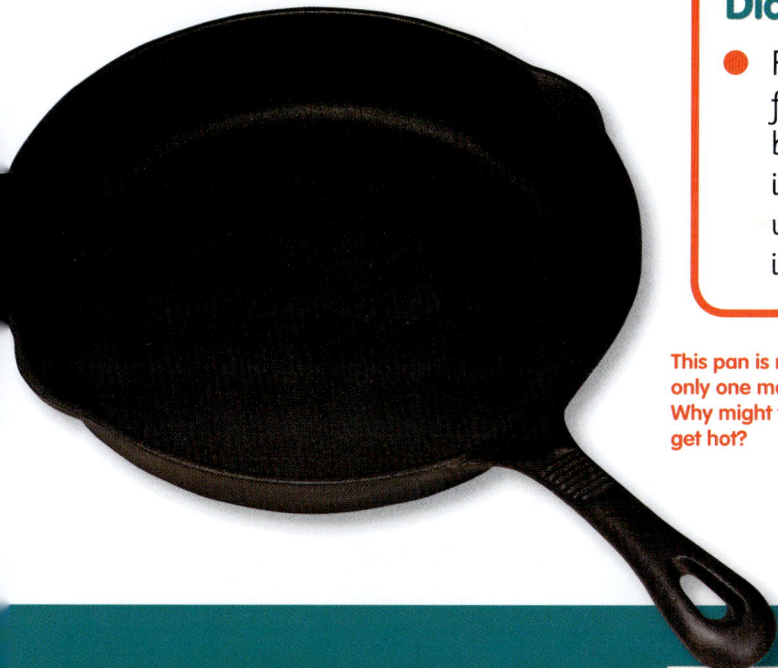

I wonder...

What makes a good thermal conductor and a good electrical conductor?

Dig deeper

Find out:
- more about temperature and heat travelling
- which way heat travels.

Did you know?

- Polar bears have two layers of fur. This traps air close to their body and keeps their body heat in. They have a thick layer of fat under their skin. Fat is a good insulator too.

This pan is made of only one material. Why might the handle get hot?

What have you learned?

- Temperature is a measure of how hot or cold things are.
- A thermometer measures temperature accurately.
- There are different kinds of thermometers.
- Objects gain or lose heat until they reach room temperature.
- **Thermal** conductors allow heat to travel through them easily and quickly.
- Thermal insulators slow the movement of heat.
- Air is a good thermal insulator; thick fabrics trap air.
- Metals are good thermal conductors.
- How to use a thermometer carefully and accurately.
- You must handle a thermometer with care.

Find out more about…

- wool and why it is used for clothes
- **molecules** cooling down.

Check-up

Maalik takes lunch to school every day. He keeps his lunch box in his classroom. The classroom is warm and there is no fridge. What could he do to keep his lunch cool?

How can Maalik keep his lunch cool?

The answer!

Remember the first question? Loft insulation is very thick with loose **fibres**. It looks like cotton wool. It has air trapped in it. Air is a good thermal insulator. The trapped air helps to insulate the house. The heat that has risen to the loft can't easily escape from the house. This makes it warmer indoors!
If the house isn't warm, then there isn't any heat to keep in. Loft insulation only keeps in the heat that is already there.

Unit 4: Separating solids and liquids

Everything in the world is made up of **matter** – the scientific word for 'stuff'. The air all around us is matter, even though we can't see it! There are three types of matter – **solids**, **liquids** and **gases**. These are called the 'states' of matter. Sometimes matter can be changed from one 'state' to another. You are going to learn about two of the states, liquids and solids, and how they can be separated. Gases come later!

What do you know?

- Some materials are natural and some are made.
- Materials have different properties.
- Heating and cooling can cause some materials to change.
- What happens to water when it is heated and cooled.
- How to use a sieve to **separate** different-sized solid particles.

Words to learn

dissolve
dissolved
filter
freeze
insoluble
liquid
melt
particle

separate
sieve
solid
solidify
soluble
solution
undissolved

Skills check

Can you...

- make careful observations and measurements?
- collect evidence to explain what you've found out?
- use your evidence to predict something you don't yet know?

Let's find out...

The river near Mansoor's school is polluted. Class 4 have cleared away all the rubbish they could find from the river and its banks. The water looks very clean and clear but fish still don't live in it. What can the problem be?

Properties of materials

Atomic Greek

About 2500 years ago, a Greek scientist had a thought. If you kept cutting a material in half, it would be too small to divide any more. He called this smallest possible particle an 'atom'. It would take millions of atoms to cover the full stop at the end of this sentence. Now that's small! All matter is made up of atoms. Different arrangements of atoms or particles make different materials. A material is either a solid or a liquid depending on how its particles are arranged. If the particles move freely then it is a gas.

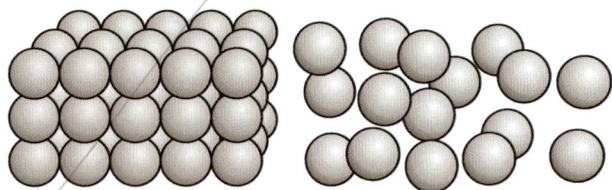

solid   liquid

Shape up

Imagine how closely fruit is packed in boxes. This is how particles in a solid are packed. Solids, like a book or block of wood, have a structure. They have a shape that's not easy to change. Even tiny pieces of solid – like sugar – have their own shape.

Get moving

Have you played in a ball pond? The balls are like particles in a liquid. They are close together but they move around each other. This is how a liquid flows.

Moving freely

Particles in gases are free to move everywhere. If you spray particles from an air freshener, you can soon smell them around the room.

Things to do

Measure water

Look at some water in a glass. You can see that the water has no shape of its own. It takes the shape of the glass. When water is poured into different containers, its volume (how much of it there is) stays the same but its shape changes.

- Find some different shaped containers. Fill them with water and see what shape the water takes.
- Look at the top of the water. You'll see that it's level. Try tipping it. What happens to the water level now?
- Liquids always have a **flat** top!

I wonder...

What solid water looks like. Maybe you know!

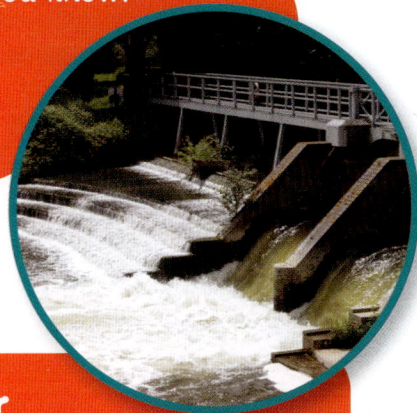

Dig deeper

Find out:
- how engineers use liquids as **lubrication**, for fuel and to make things move in **hydraulic** machines
- how the properties of liquids are useful to us.

Did you know?

- Long ago, scientists called alchemists tried to make gold from other materials. But it's impossible!
- Most metals are solid but **mercury** is liquid at room temperature.
- The temperature on Neptune is so low that no liquids can exist.

Solids and liquids

Your challenge

● Identify solids, liquids and solids that act like liquids.

The crew of the Starship Venture need to find a cure for a deadly disease on planet Xerex. But Captain Berzelius has a problem. All of the labels on his first aid kit have been removed.

What to do

How could the Captain recognize the correct medicine? How could the Doctor describe it to him?

Look carefully at a collection of materials. Think how you could group them.

Could you pour your material? Is it a solid or a liquid? What happens when you mix it with water? What does it smell like?

Remember, the crew can't taste their materials. They could be dangerous!

We have a problem, Doctor. A **spy** has removed all of the labels.

Don't worry Captain! The Xerelian disease is easily cured. Just find the medicine labelled D51.

Describe D51 to me and I'll try to find it!

The wrong medicine might kill someone!

What you need

● A selection of materials
● A hand lens or magnifying glass
● A beaker
● Water
● A spoon
● A measuring cylinder.

What to check

Now try it yourselves.

● What tests will you do to decide which materials are solid and which are liquid?
● What about materials that have both solid and liquid properties (like a gel)?
● Will you keep the quantities of your materials the same?

What did you find?

The Doctor gave Captain Berzelius a set of instructions to sort out the materials. First, he needed to sort the liquids from the solids. He needed to do several tests. Here is his first set of results:

Can you do better?

- How good is your evidence?
- Make a general rule about your results.
- Make a key to identify your materials?

Mystery material	Has its own shape (or can be piled up)?	Keeps a level surface when tipped?	Forms drips when poured?	Solid or liquid?
1	yes	no	no	solid
2	no	yes	yes	liquid
3	yes	can't be poured	no	solid
4	no	yes	yes	liquid
5	yes	can't be poured	no	solid
6	yes	no	no	solid
7	no	yes	yes	liquid
8	yes	no	no	solid
9	no	yes	yes	liquid
10	yes	no	no	solid

- Captain Berzelius sorted which materials were solids and which were liquids. Was he right?
- What happens to the liquids if we change the containers they're in?
- What other tests separate liquids from solids?

Now predict

The Captain discovered that some solids could behave like liquids if they had tiny particles.

- How would you group jelly, custard, toothpaste, tomato ketchup, whipped cream and hair gel? Are they solids, liquids or something else?
- Have you enough evidence to find the medicine?

Changing materials

Your challenge

- Investigate how materials can be changed by heating and cooling.
- Investigate if some changes can be reversed.

Can we put the ice cream for my party on the table yet?

*Not yet. You don't want it to **melt**, do you? Let's put those chocolate biscuits in the fridge until your friends arrive.*

But nothing else is melting.

What would happen to the ice cream if it were left on the table for a long time? Why did Mum want to put the chocolate biscuits back into the fridge?

What to do

After her party Riya decided to find out more about how things change from solids to liquids and back again. She put small pieces of food in cake cases and floated them on hot water.

What you need

- Butter, margarine, solid vegetable fat, milk chocolate, dark chocolate, jelly cube, ice cube
- A bowl
- Hot tap water
- Cake cases
- Small paper flags.

What to check

Now try it yourselves.

- What are you going to measure?
- How will you decide if something has melted?
- How are you going to check and record your results?

I'm using hot water from the tap.

I'll cut the same-sized piece from each food.

What did you find?

Riya chose some foods to test. As the foods heated on the hot water, she wrote down what she saw:

Test material	What happened when it was heated
butter	melted quickly
margarine	melted slowly
vegetable fat	melted quickly
milk chocolate	melted quickly
dark chocolate	melted slowly
jelly cube	melted really slowly
ice cube	melted fastest

Riya left the foods to cool. She noticed that the butter, margarine, chocolate and fat became solid again. But the ice cube was still liquid. She put it in the fridge but it still didn't **solidify**.

Can you do better?

- How good is your evidence?
- How many more foods can you find to test?

Not everything needs to be put in a cold place to become solid. Look at the wax in this candle. As it heats, it becomes liquid and runs down the candle.

And it turns to solid wax again! But it doesn't have to be in a really cold place. Cool!

Now predict

- Riya's mum is baking a cake. She gets the margarine out of the fridge. She heats it in the microwave oven for a few seconds. Why does she do that?
- What would happen if she put the margarine back in the fridge?

Things to learn

- Mixtures of solids can sometimes be separated.
- Mixtures of solids and liquids can sometimes be separated.
- The different properties of materials can help us to separate them.

All mixed up

When two or more materials are mixed together we get a mixture. Look at a packet of soup mix. It might contain dried pasta, beans, vegetables and spices. Some mixtures are harder to recognize. Mayonnaise is a mixture of oil and eggs but it just looks like one creamy substance. How many mixtures can you think of?

Sieve it

A **sieve** will hold back anything with particles bigger than the size of its holes. Different sieves have different sizes of holes. You can separate large (coarse) particles and small (fine) particles.

We can also use sieves to separate some solids from liquids. At home, you might have a special sieve called a colander. This separates vegetables from the water they have been cooked or cleaned in.

Paper sieves

Sometimes we need to separate very small solid particles mixed with liquids. A normal sieve might not do the job. But we could try paper. Paper has very small holes and is like a mini-sieve. Liquids can pass through but tiny particles of solids are left behind. This is called **filtering**.

Look at a tea bag or a coffee filter paper with a hand lens. What can you see?

I wonder...

Khaled squeezes some oranges but he gets **pips** and bits of orange **pulp** in his juice. How can he separate them from the juice?

Things to do

Make a mixture

- Mix together different-sized dry solids. Try rice and salt or **lentils**, sugar and pasta shapes. How many sieves will you need to separate them? Which sieve will you use first?

Filter it out

Which materials make the best filters?

- Try different papers and cloths. Filter some muddy water. Use a funnel to help you. Which do you think will work best? Look at your materials closely with a hand lens. Does that give you any clues? Which filter is fastest and which is slowest?

Dig deeper

Find out:
- more about what filters are made from
- how we use filters in cars and at home.

Did you know?

- The hairs in your nose are a filter. They stop dirt and dust getting into your lungs.
- **Gunpowder** is a mixture of yellow sulphur and charcoal. It was first discovered in China over 3000 years ago.
- Coffee can be filtered to take out the coffee solids.

Things to learn

- The same material can exist at different temperatures.
- Heating a solid can make it change to a liquid.
- Cooling a liquid can make it change to a solid.
- Water exists in three states – solid, liquid and gas.
- Heating or cooling water changes its state.

Turning up the heat

Many materials can be both solids and liquids. It depends on their temperature. Metal is usually solid. It becomes liquid if it is hot enough. The Earth's core is so hot that rocks are liquid. This liquid rock, called lava, erupts from volcanoes.

Disappearing acts

When some solids are mixed with water they seem to disappear. But do they? Sugar **dissolves** in water perfectly. It spreads throughout the water to make a sugar **solution**. Could you use a filter to get the sugar back?

Water, water everywhere

We find water on Earth in all three states. We find it as water, ice and **water vapour**. Investigate what happens if you put water in the freezer, then put it in a fridge until it melts and then put it back into the freezer.

The freezer is below 0°C. The water freezes into ice, but white spirit stays liquid

The fridge is just above 0°C. The ice melts back to water, but butter stays solid

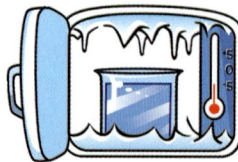

What do you think will happen if the water is put back into the freezer?

Things to do

Water marks

Bottled water has mineral salts dissolved in it. These change its taste.

- Pour some different mineral waters onto some clear saucers. Try tap water too. Leave the water to dry up in the Sun, then see what's left behind. You should see a fine powder. These are the chemicals that were dissolved in the water. Look at them through a microscope. Where has the water gone? It has evaporated. It has become water vapour.

Salt rings left after the water has evaporated

I wonder...

In some countries ponds freeze in winter but the sea rarely freezes. Why is that?

Kitchen chemistry

Liquids dissolve in water too. When you make a drink of orange **cordial**, you're dissolving the cordial in the water. Do all liquids dissolve in water?

- Try mixing some small amounts of oil, vinegar, milk, syrup, washing-up liquid or fruit juice with water. Record what you see.

Dig deeper

Find out:
- more about melting and freezing
- what happens when you freeze salty water.

Did you know?

- Almost all of the world's water is liquid. Only one 50th of the water is ice.
- The Ice Hotel in Sweden is the world's biggest igloo. It is made completely from ice and is rebuilt every December.

Dissolving solids

On the Starship Venture, Captain Berzelius is still trying to find medicine D51.

What to do

The Captain poured 100 ml of cold water into six beakers. Then he mixed a level teaspoon of each solid with the water. He stirred each mixture for exactly one minute. He let the mixture settle. He looked at the result. What do you think? Decide what to measure and how you'll record your results.

What you need

- A selection of safe white solids
- A measuring cylinder
- Transparent beakers
- A teaspoon
- A funnel
- Filter paper
- A magnifying glass or hand lens
- A seconds timer
- A **petri dish** or saucer.

We've separated all the medicines, Doctor. I've got six white solids here.

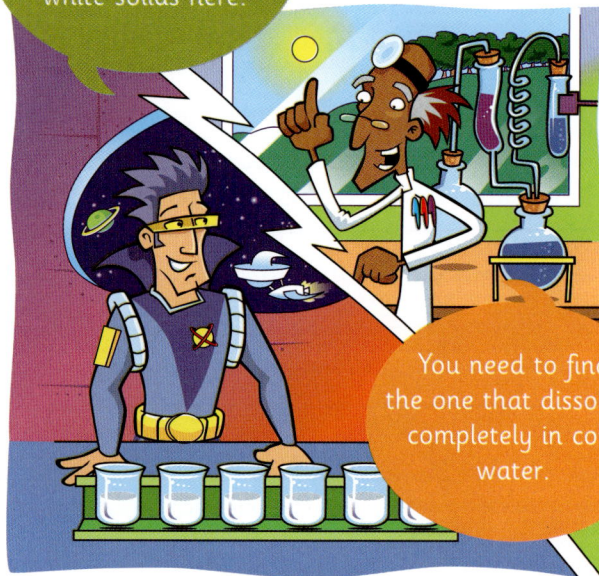

You need to find the one that dissolves completely in cold water.

What to check

Now try it yourselves.

- What are you going to measure?
- How will you know when your substance has dissolved?
- How many times will you repeat the investigation? Why is this a good idea?
- How will you keep the test fair?

What did you find?

The Captain tested the six solids and made a table of his results:

Sample substance	Appearance after one minute when mixed with cold water
1	Turns water cloudy, white powder sinks to the bottom of the beaker.
2	Some of the solid disappears but most stays in **lumps**.
3	Solid sinks to bottom of beaker.
4	Some frothing. Most of the solid remains undissolved.
5	Solid disappears completely.
6	Solid dissolves but turns liquid white.

- Make a chart of your results. You could use a computer program to help you.
- Which sample is medicine D51?

We did it Doctor! The crew is saved!

You'll be in space for another month, Captain. You may need those medicines you tested.

Is there any way we can get them back out of the water?

Can you do better?
- How good is your evidence?
- What would you do differently if you did this again?
- Would the temperature of the water make a difference?

Now predict
- How can the Captain get the solids out of the water? Can he get them all back? What about the ones that have dissolved?
- Mix some sand and some salt in water. Think about how you could get both the salt and the sand back.

Unit 4: Review

What have you learned?

- Everything in the world is made of materials.
- Materials can be solid, liquid or gas.
- Heating or cooling materials can make them change.
- Mixing materials can make them change.
- When a solid changes to a liquid it melts.
- When a liquid changes to a solid it freezes.
- When a liquid evaporates, it becomes a gas.
- Melting and freezing happen at different temperatures for different substances.
- Some changes can be **reversed**; others are **irreversible**.
- Materials can be separated in different ways.
- Sieving can separate mixtures of solids.
- Some materials cannot dissolve in a liquid; these are **insoluble**.
- Some materials can dissolve in a liquid; these are **soluble**.
- Insoluble solids can be separated from liquids by sieving or filtering.
- Soluble materials can be separated from liquids by evaporation.

Find out more about...

- how water is recycled
- how sea water is desalinated.

Check-up

Hassan and Jamal have accidentally mixed rice, salt and flour together. They want to separate them again. What should they do?

The answer!

Do you remember the question about the polluted river? Even though water may look clean and clear, it may have chemicals dissolved in it that we can't see. Although the students have removed the rubbish, they have not been able to remove the dissolved chemicals in the water. If we stop **dumping** chemicals in rivers, eventually they will become clean.

Unit 5: Gases around us

If you visit a fairground, you might see someone selling balloons that float in the air. If they are let go they rise into the sky and get blown away.

You can often smell food at a fairground! When you come off the rides you are breathless. You take in more oxygen and breathe out more carbon dioxide. All these experiences involve gases. But what is a gas?

What do you know?

- There are solids, liquids and gases.
- Solids, liquids and gases are different states.
- Volume is the amount of space that something takes up.
- Oxygen and carbon dioxide are gases.

Words to learn

air
carbon dioxide
chlorine
condensation
evaporation
gas
helium
hydrogen
natural gas
oxygen
particles

Skills check

Can you...
- measure the volume of a liquid?
- make careful observations?

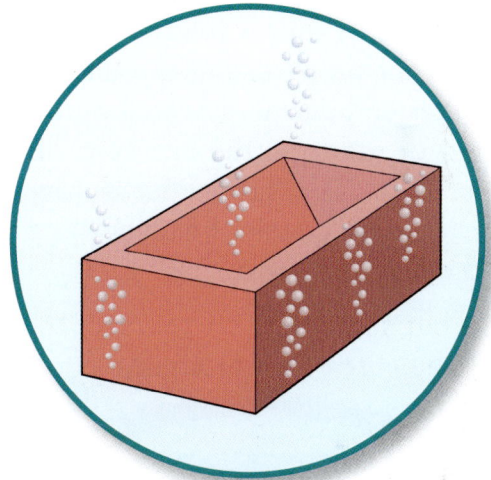

Let's find out...

If you put a house brick in water, bubbles come out of it. What are these bubbles? Where have they come from?

Solids, liquids and gases

Things to learn
- There are differences between solids and liquids.
- Air has weight.

Set in its ways

A solid has a definite shape. Or does it? Is a powder, like flour, a solid? What about sand? Is that a solid? You need to know the properties of a solid. Test a powder and decide. Look carefully at flour or sand. Do the bits keep their shape? If so, it's a solid. Pour it. Maybe it's a liquid? A powder behaves like a liquid as well as like a solid!

Carry out some tests on powders to find out if they are solids or liquids.

When it's windy you can see the effects of the air moving

Wind

Some seeds are dispersed by the wind. What must seeds be like to be carried on the wind?

The wind is **air** moving from one place to another. You can feel it on your face when you run or through an open window in a moving car. Aeroplanes need air to give them 'lift' so they can take off and stay in the air. And we need air to breathe!

Some solids pour like liquids but don't have a flat top

Things to do

Gas has mass

Balance a wire coathanger on a pencil from its hook. Does the coathanger hang level? Add Blu-tack until it does. Now it is a very sensitive balance.

- Blow up a balloon. Tie a knot in the end to stop the air escaping. Use a small piece of sticky tape to stick the balloon to one end of the coat hanger. Stick the same sort of balloon that hasn't been blown up to the other end of the coathanger.
- What happens? Can you explain why? Why do the balloons have to be the same in every way? What does this investigation tell you about air?

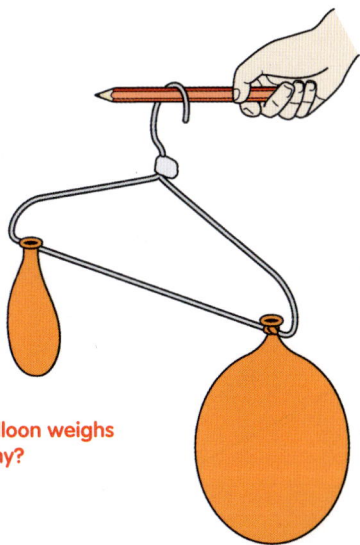

Which balloon weighs more? Why?

I wonder...

Why is it important that air is transparent, **odourless** and colourless? What difference would it make if it wasn't?

Dig deeper

Find out:
- more about solids and liquids
- what **capillary action** is
- about **surface tension**.

Did you know?

- Gases have weight – a blown-up balloon weighs more than a flat one.
- Some gases – including **hydrogen** and **helium** – are lighter than air. Hot air is lighter than cold air. This is why gas balloons and hot air balloons rise.
- Gases fill the space available to them.

Air around us

Things to learn

- Air is often mixed with solids and liquids.
- The spaces in solids are filled with a gas, often air.

What is matter?

Everything is made of stuff called matter, but what is matter? All matter is made of very tiny particles. Modern microscopes can show us some of these particles. Gases are made up of particles like these, too.

Honeycomb chocolate

Honeycomb chocolate

Have you ever eaten a **honeycomb** chocolate bar? What does it look like on the inside? The chocolate is solid, but what is in the holes? Are they empty? No – the holes are filled with gas!

How would you describe a honeycomb chocolate bar to someone who has never seen one?

What other foods have this 'holey' structure? Are there other things with the same structure?

Full of fizz

If you pour yourself a glass of lemonade what do you see? If you shake the bottle first what happens? The bubbles are made of a gas called **carbon dioxide**. The carbon dioxide is dissolved in the lemonade. It can only escape when the bottle is opened. Lemonade is 'flat' without it. Which way do the bubbles move? What does this tell you about how heavy the carbon dioxide is?

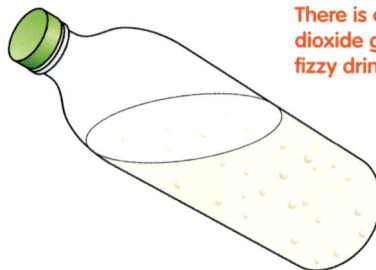

There is carbon dioxide gas in fizzy drinks

Things to do

Investigate sand and water

- Put some sand in a beaker. Measure its volume. Add an equal volume of water. What do you expect the final volume to be?
- What happens? Can you explain why? Why would it be a good idea to repeat the investigation?
- Does the same thing happen with any volume of sand and water?

Dig deeper

Find out:
- more about the importance of air
- why the Earth and all living things need air. What gas in the air do they all need?

We live at the bottom of a 'sea' of air that is called the atmosphere

I wonder...

If you looked at a piece of kitchen towel under a microscope what would you see?

Did you know?

- There isn't any air in space or on the Moon. This is why there isn't any life on the Moon.
- A horror film was advertised with the words, 'In space, no one can hear you scream!' That's true. Outer space has no air. Sound travels through air – but it can't travel through an airless vacuum.

Air in the soil

Your challenge

- Discover what worms and other soil creatures need to live.
- Make a prediction.
- Begin to think about the need for repeated measurements.

What to do

A worm gets its food and the air that it needs to breathe from soil. Tightly packed soil is hard for a worm to move through. Class 4 wants to set up a wormery. Which type of soil is best for worms?

The class knows that worms need air. But which soil holds the most? Here are their suggestions about how to find out. Which would you use?

I'm glad I'm out of that clay.

Not just that! I couldn't breathe properly.

Why, was it hard eating?

You could pour enough water to cover the soil up and measure how much water it takes.

You could look at each soil type under a microscope and count the number of gaps.

You could drop each soil type in water and look at the bubbles coming out.

What you need

- Different types of soil
- A measuring cylinder
- Water.

What to check

Now try it yourselves.

- How will Class 4 know which soil has the most air spaces?
- What will they need to measure?
- What will they keep the same?
- How much can they trust their evidence?
- How can they make their evidence more reliable?
- Why might they repeat the investigation with more soil?

What did you find?

The students put soil in a measuring cylinder up to the 50 ml mark. Then they added water until the soil and water reached the 100 ml mark. Here are their results.

Soil type	Volume of water needed (ml)	
	First try	Second try
sand	80	78
clay	95	99
compost	65	68
pond	85	87

- If you were drawing a graph of these results, which set of results would you choose? Explain why. What would be fairer?
- Draw a graph of your results. Should it be a line graph or a bar chart? What do your results tell you? Which soil would be easiest for worms to burrow through? How can you tell?

Can you do better?

- The group's results weren't exactly the same each time. Why do you think this was? If they tried this again what results would you expect to see?

Earth worms rely on the air in the soil

Now predict

- If a soil has lots of air spaces in it, would you expect to find lots of worms in the soil? Would it let water through easily?
- If an area of your garden gets waterlogged what type of soil would you expect to find?

Different gases

Gas-tastic!

Floating balloons at a fairground don't have air in them. They are filled with a gas called helium. Helium is lighter than air. Helium-filled balloons float in air.

Butane gas is used for cooking. You can buy large cylinders for home or small cylinders for use when camping.

Neon is a gas in the brightly coloured flashing lights in shop windows. It's also used in **fluorescent** lights in the classroom.

Air is a mixture of gases. Without the gases oxygen and carbon dioxide, life on Earth would not exist.

In some places gas is delivered to homes in cylinders

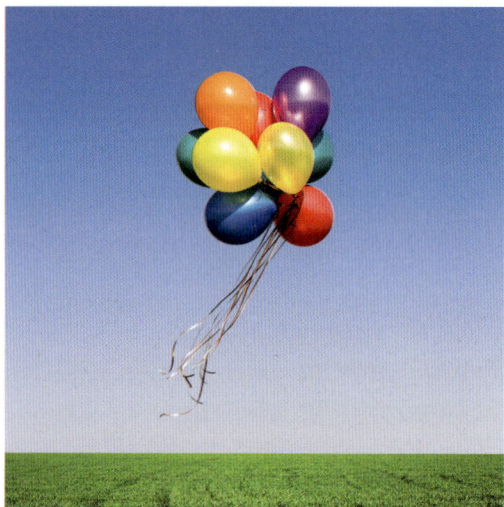
Helium balloons float

Gas attack

Some gases are harmful as well as helpful. **Chlorine** is used as an antiseptic in swimming pools. It kills harmful micro-organisms. But when it isn't in water, chlorine gas is poisonous.

Carbon dioxide is used by plants to make food and oxygen. There is more carbon dioxide in the air we breathe out than in the air we breathe in. But too much carbon dioxide in a closed space kills us.

Carbon monoxide is a poisonous gas produced by cars and when things burn.

Things to do

Gas disaster!

Professor Vapour is a little confused. He has been investigating some gases. Unfortunately, he had a small explosion. Most of his notes have been burned. He has collected all he can. Now he needs some help working out what they mean.

- Your teacher has his notes. Work out what gases he was testing and some of their properties.

I wonder…

Is oxygen ever harmful? Can you have too much of it?

Dig deeper

Find out:
- more about what gases we use
- why hydrogen is used to **inflate** hot air balloons
- how some gases, like butane, are stored.

Did you know?

- Some gases glow when you pass an electric current through them. We see different colours with different gases.
- Laughing gas (nitrous oxide) got its name from making people laugh, but only if they breathed in a small amount. If they breathed in more, it sent them to sleep. Laughing gas was used as an **anaesthetic** by dentists.

Moving gases

Things to learn

- We smell things when they enter our nose.
- All liquids evaporate to form gases.
- Gases move from place to place easily.

Mmmmm!

Imagine walking past a café. What can you smell? Food, of course! But how do you smell it? Your nose detects the tiny particles of the food in the air and your brain tells you what you are smelling. Smelling food can make you feel hungry!

Now you see it...

Some perfumes and lotions feel cold on your skin. When you put them on your warm skin, they **evaporate**. Particles in the air enter your nose. You can smell the perfume.

What would happen if you left the perfume bottle open?

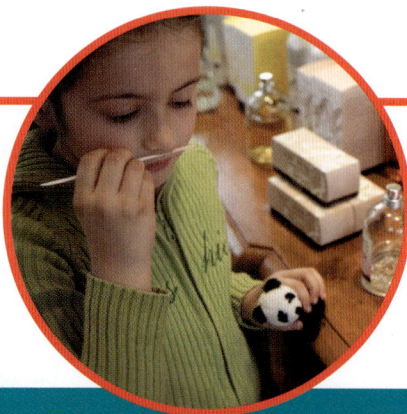

...now you don't

The particles evaporate quickly. They leave the surface and move into the air. Your warm skin speeds up the **evaporation**.

Particles in the perfume move from the bottle to your nose

What will happen to the rainwater when the Sun comes out?

Things to do

Rain and shine

If you go outside after rain you'll see lots of puddles. If the Sun comes out what happens to the puddles? Does this happen immediately?

- Find a large puddle just after it has stopped raining and the Sun has come out. Draw a chalk line around the edge of it. What will happen to the puddle after one hour in the sunshine?
- Go back to the puddle after one hour. Draw a chalk line around its edge again. Is it the same size as last time? Do this every hour until the puddle has gone completely. Where does the water go?

I wonder…

Natural gas – the gas some people cook with – doesn't have its own smell. The smell is put in by the gas company. Why? What happens when gas leaks? Why is it important to smell it?

Dig deeper

Find out:
- how your nose works and how you smell with it
- if other animals can sense different smells.

Did you know?

- If you hold your nose, you can't taste food well. Onion and apple taste very similar when your nose is closed!
- When clothes dry on a line, the water in them is evaporating. It moves from the clothes to the air.

Things to learn

- Describe the differences between solids, liquids and gases.
- Describe the properties of solids, liquids and gases.

What a state!

There are three states of matter – solid, liquid and gas. They all have different properties. The water below is **changing state**.

Find three states of matter in this picture

The picture shows ice cubes and liquid water with water vapour above. This is matter in all three states. Which is the solid and which the liquid? What will happen to the ice cube if you leave it on a table?

'Steam' is not really water gas. It is water vapour – particles of liquid water in the air. Water is a gas only when it is hotter than its boiling point – hotter than 100°C. True water gas is invisible.

Squidgy

Are solids **squidgy**? You might think some of them are, like sponges. But what properties does a solid have that allows you to squash it? What sort of solid objects can you squash?

Do you remember that all matter is made of particles? These particles are very tightly packed in a solid – there's no room to squash them close together. In a gas, the particles are very far apart, so there is lots of space between them. They can be squashed into these spaces.

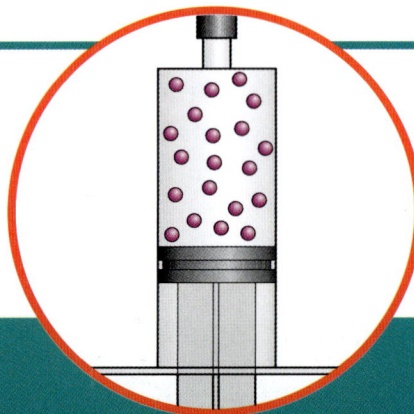

There are spaces betwe[en] gas particles [so] you can squa[sh] gases in a syringe

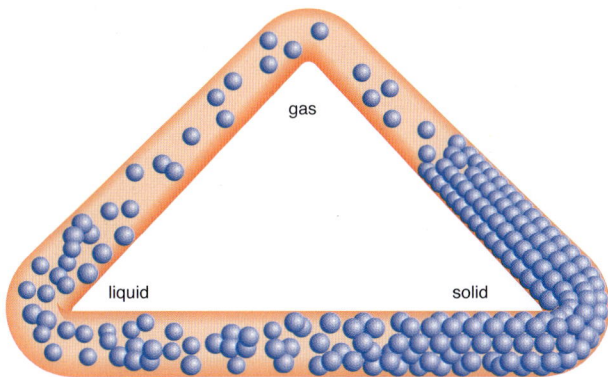

Gas particles move more freely than particles in solids or liquids

Things to do

What's the difference?

You know there are differences between solids, liquids and gases, but what tests can you do to prove them?

- How can you prove that a liquid needs a container and takes it shape from it?
- How can you prove that a liquid and a solid keep the same volume when they change shape?
- How do you know that liquids and gases flow from place to place?
- Can you ever squash solids?
- Draw a picture of the tests you could use to prove your ideas.

Dig deeper

Find out:
- about the differences between the three states of matter
- how you can make a substance change its state. What are you giving to the particles?

Did you know?

- If it is cold enough, even air can freeze.
- Water is almost the only material to get bigger when it freezes.
- Some gases are so heavy that they can be poured just like a liquid.

What have you learned?

- Gases are materials and have weight.
- The spaces in solids are filled with a gas, often air.
- Gases change shape and flow from place to place.
- We smell things when they enter our nose.
- All liquids evaporate to form gases.
- There are lots of different gases.
- Some gases are useful to us, some are harmful.

Find out more about...

- the rare fourth state of matter!
- how the particles in water are special.

Check-up

Aisha is looking after her baby brother. She smells something nasty. She asks her dad, in the kitchen, if he can smell it. He says he can't. Aisha discovers the smell is coming from the baby's nappy! She changes his nappy and washes it. Her dad hangs it outside to dry.

- Why can Aisha smell the nappy before her dad?
- What will happen to the water in the washed nappy?

The answer!

Remember the very first question? House bricks are fairly solid things. But they have small spaces all through them. Air is trapped in these spaces. When you put a brick in water the water drives out the air and it rises as bubbles.
So when you see a bubble you are seeing air – or at least, the space it takes up in water!

Unit 6: Electricity

When you go home you might turn on the lights, have a shower, dry your hair with a hair dryer, watch television or play a computer game. You might take something out of the fridge and warm it up in the microwave. Without electricity, few of these things would be possible. Think what your world would be like without it!

What do you know?

- Electrical items use either mains electricity or batteries.
- Electricity won't flow unless there is a complete **circuit**.
- The names of things – **components** – you can use in a simple circuit.
- Mains electricity can be dangerous if you don't use it properly.

Skills check

Can you...

- make careful observations and measurements?
- collect evidence and decide how good it is?
- use your evidence to explain what you found out?

Large cities such as Dubai use electricty widely

Words to learn

attract	current
battery	electrical
bulb	insulator
buzzer	magnet
break	motor
cell	repel
circuit	switch
conduct	terminal
conductor	**voltage**

Let's find out...

Has your home got a hallway? Maybe there is a light on the **landing**. You can switch it on from the bottom of the stairs – and switch it off when you get to the top. One lamp, two switches and only one source of electricity. How can that work?

Simple circuits

Things to learn

- A circuit needs a source of electricity.
- A complete circuit is needed for a device to work.
- Some materials conduct electricity and others do not.
- The scientific name for a battery is a cell.

It's electrifying!

Electricity is a very useful form of energy. It can be changed into other types of energy like light, heat and movement. It flows along wires that can be twisted to go anywhere. Imagine if your television worked on gas. You would need to attach a gas pipe to it!

Everything in the world is made up of tiny particles called atoms. If we looked at an atom through a really powerful microscope we would see that it contained even smaller particles called electrons. Electrons move from one atom to another. This moving stream of electrons creates an electric **current**.

Imagine if you could see a **bird's-eye view** of a rainforest. All you would see is a mass of green trees. If you came closer you could see other things, like monkeys swinging through the branches. Electrons are a bit like the monkeys – we can't see them in electrical wire but they are moving through it.

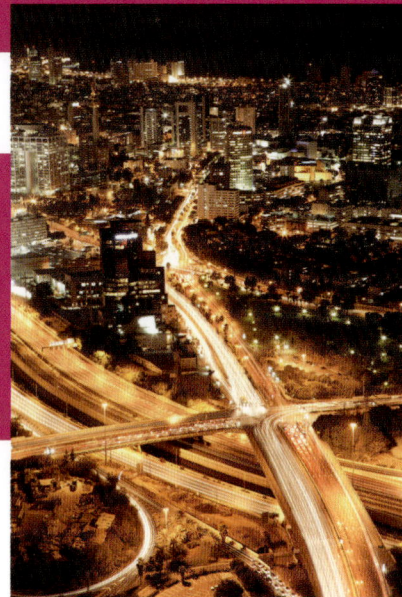

Round and round

A circuit is the path electricity takes when it flows. Electricity cannot (usually) jump gaps. The different components in the circuit must all be connected to each other to make a complete circuit. This is needed for electricity to flow. If a circuit had any breaks in it, the electricty wouldn't be able to flow round it.

Making it work

Electricity comes from a source. The source might be a **battery** (or **cell**) or **mains** electricity from a socket in the wall. A battery acts like a pump. It provides the push to drive the electrons round the circuit. Mains electricity has a very big push and can be very dangerous. Never play with mains electricity!

Things to do

Build a battery

Chemicals in a battery push electrons round a complete circuit. An Italian scientist called Alessandro Volta invented the first battery in the eighteenth century. His 'Voltaic pile' was made by stacking up discs of zinc, copper and leather soaked in salt water.

- Make a Voltaic pile with discs of aluminium foil, copper coins and circles of blotting paper soaked in salty water. Attach a wire to a copper coin and build up layers of foil, paper and coins. End with a wire attached to a foil disc.

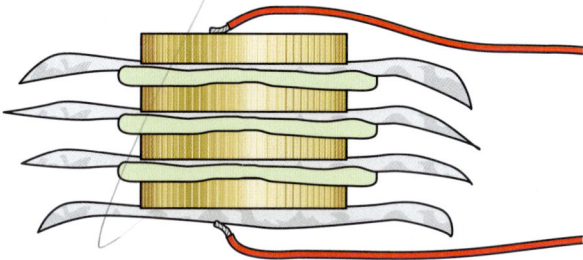

I wonder…

Why is a fire-fighter's helmet made of fibreglass and not metal? Why do electricians use wooden ladders?

Baffling batteries

Batteries come in many shapes and sizes. How many can you find? All batteries are marked with a + and a −. These are the positive (+) and negative (−) **terminals** of the battery. Electricity flows from the negative terminal of the battery to the positive terminal.

Dig deeper

Find out:
- about the genius Michael Faraday and how his electrical discoveries changed the world.

Did you know?

- Correctly, a single cylindrical battery should be called a 'cell'. Two or more is a 'battery'. Bigger batteries are harmful of course – and you can get a nasty **jolt** from a 12V car battery. Even a small battery will tickle your tongue!
- Because there was no way of measuring electricity 300 years ago, scientists used their bodies as a test machine. They observed how far electricity went up their arm – or how far it went along a row of people holding hands.

Investigating circuits

Your challenge

- Investigate how to make a bulb light up.

I've got some batteries, bulbs, wires and bulb holders. Take what you think you'll need to make one bulb light up.

Just put your wires on the bulb. Then the electricity comes out of the battery and into the bulb to light it up.

You need two wires. It won't work with just one. Do they have to be different colours?

I'm going to light my bulb. I just need a battery and a wire.

What to do

- Decide how to construct your circuit. Try to make your **bulb** light with just one wire.
- Do you need a bulb holder? Does it matter which way round the battery is?
- Can you change anything about your circuit to make the bulb switch on and off when you want it to? What would you need to add?

Take a closer look at the bulb. Work out how the electricity flows through it

What you need

- Batteries
- Bulbs and holders
- Wires
- A magnifying glass or hand lens.

What to check

Now try it yourselves.

- How can you make your bulb light in more than one way?
- If your circuit isn't working, what will you check?
- How will you record your investigation?

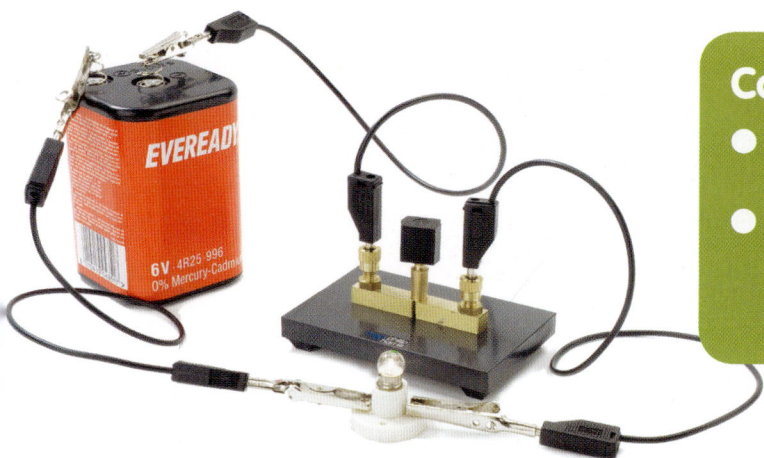

Can you do better?

- Make up a rule that must be followed to make a circuit work.
- Ask your friends to construct a circuit from the diagram you drew.

What did you find?

The students drew diagrams of their results. Some of their circuits worked but others didn't.

- Look at their diagrams. Decide which bulbs would light and which ones wouldn't.

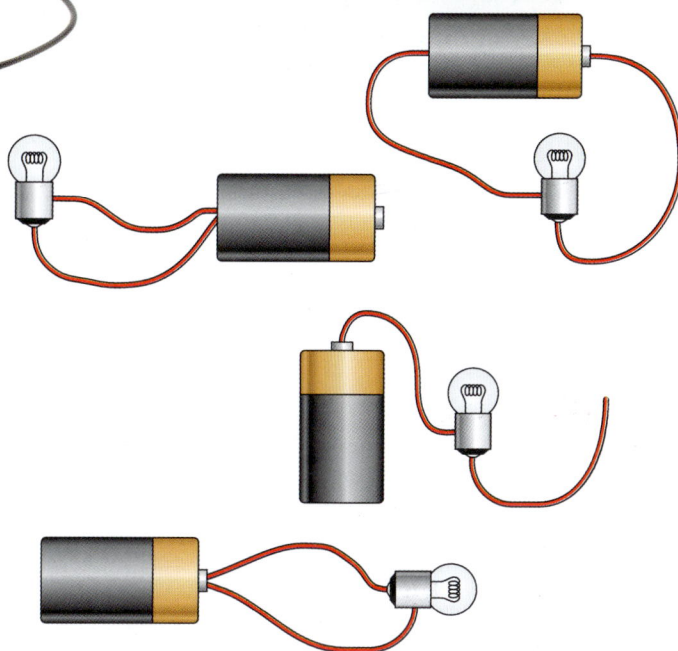

Now predict

- A torch usually has more than one cell inside it. How would you draw a circuit diagram for a torch?
- Box-shaped batteries are made of two or more cells. How are the cells connected together?

Conductors and insulators

Your challenge

- Find out which materials conduct electricity.

We shouldn't use fishing rods near overhead wires. Electricity can be really dangerous.

Electricity only flows through metal, doesn't it? My rod is made of carbon fibre. Electricity won't flow through it, will it?

I don't know. But we are not safe here. Let's test your rod when we get home.

DANGER!

What to do

Make a circuit with a break in it, like the one below:

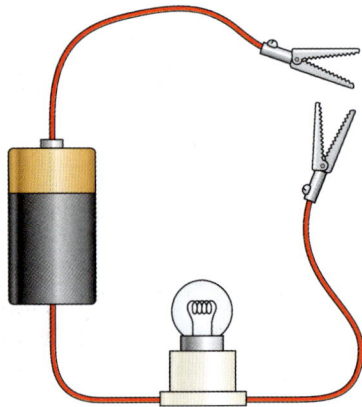

We call this sort of circuit an open circuit. Put some test materials in the gap. If the bulb lights up, you have made a complete circuit. Your material is an electrical conductor. Electricity flows easily through an electrical conductor. If the bulb doesn't light up, you have tested an electrical insulator. The electricity will not flow easily through an electrical insulator.

Don't test watches or anything electrical!

What you need

- A battery
- A bulb or buzzer
- Three wires
- A selection of materials to test
- A pencil, sharpened at both end.

What to check

Now try each material yourselves.

- Predict which materials will be conductors.

What did you find?

This chart shows Layla's predictions:

Materials	Conductor? Yes/no
metal paper clip	yes
birthday card	no
pencil eraser	no
plastic toothbrush	no
steel scissors	yes
silver necklace	yes
aluminium foil	yes

Layla predicted the results of her tests correctly.

- Use your own results or Layla's. Make a general rule about materials that are good conductors and those that are not.
- Make a list of where we use electrical conductors and insulators at home and at school.
- Why is it important to insulate electrical wire?

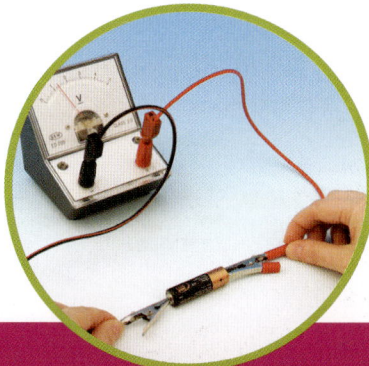

Your fishing rod is made out of carbon – it conducts electricity.

With electricity that strong, it could have killed you!

I thought only metals did that. If I had touched the electric cables with the fishing rod ...

Can you do better?

- Now test pencil 'lead'. Pencil leads are a material called carbon.
- What do you notice about the brightness of your bulb?
- What difference does this make to your general rule?

Now predict

The wooden part of the pencil is an insulator. The pencil 'lead' is a conductor. Not a good conductor – but still a conductor.

- Try pencil leads of different lengths. What do you think is happening?
- Are any liquids conductors? Why are there few switches in a bathroom?

Designing switches

Your challenge

- Design a switch to operate components in a circuit.

This is hopeless! I can't see when it's raining! The clothes are soaked.

I've got an idea! I'll invent a battery-powered alarm to tell you when it's raining.

Omar's mum works at home. She has an office with no windows, which sometimes causes problems.

What to do

Omar built his mum a rain detector alarm. It looked like this:

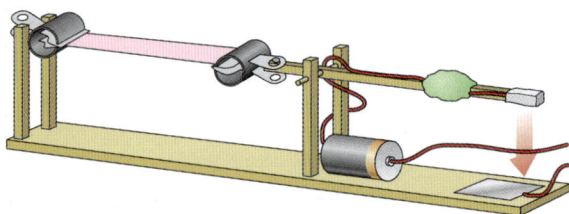

When it rained, the tissue paper got wet and tore apart. This made the see-saw arm fall onto a piece of cooking foil. The circuit was complete and a buzzer sounded in his mum's office.

You could build a rain detector or use an interesting **switch** to control a circuit for something else. Here are some ideas:

Make an alarm so you know when someone's coming into your room!

Make a pad to detect a mouse walking across it.

Make a burglar alarm to protect a gold bar.

Doorbells are no good if you're deaf. Make something to tell deaf people that they have a visitor.

What you need

- Wires
- A motor
- Buzzers
- Foil
- Balsa wood
- Split pins
- Bulbs
- Batteries
- A selection of **junk** modelling materials.

What to check

Now try it yourselves.

- Where will you put your switch?
- Does it matter where it goes in the circuit?
- What do you think will happen?

What did you find?

Omar investigated different types of switches. Here are some of them.

- How do you think they work?
- Where do you think they are used?
- What do they control?

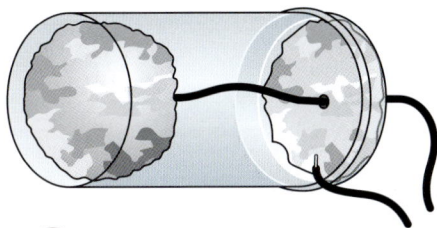

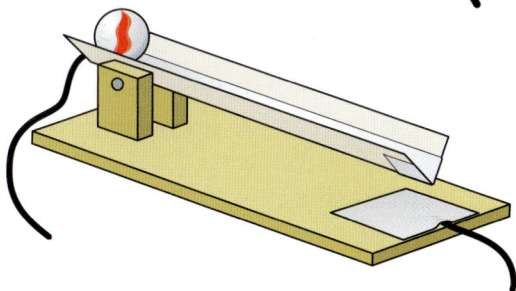

Can you do better?

- Some switches are on/off switches. Some switches need pressing to keep them on.
- Draw a diagram of a circuit with the best switch so that someone else could build it.
- Why is this the best switch for the job?

Now predict

Safia loves to read but her mum is always telling her off! She enjoys her stories so much that she doesn't notice when it starts to get dark. Safia's mum is worried that she'll hurt her eyes.

- What can Safia build to switch the light on as it gets darker? You could use a computer and a light sensor to help you.
- How could Safia make a light that switched on when she got up at night?

Brighter bulbs

Your challenge

- **Alter** the brightness of a bulb in a circuit.
- Alter the volume of a buzzer in a circuit.
- Alter the speed of a motor in a circuit.
- Plan a fair test.

My car's no good. The bulbs are too **dim** and you can hardly hear the horn. Maybe the bulbs and the buzzer need different circuits.

You need a bigger battery! You should add more batteries. Then the bulbs will be brighter.

Zafar has made a model car. It has two bulbs for headlights and a buzzer for the horn, all powered by a battery.

You could add more bulbs to see what that does to the brightness.

What to do

How can Zafar get brighter bulbs? How can he make his buzzer work well? Make up a circuit for him. What will you change?

I wonder what happens if you make the wires longer.

Decide what you will observe or measure. Remember to make only one change at a time. You could use these ideas. Or think of a change of your own.

You could add more batteries to make the bulbs brighter.

I wonder what makes electric motors go fast and slow?

You could try the buzzer in its own circuit.

What you need

- Batteries
- Bulbs
- A buzzer
- An electric motor
- Connecting wires
- A light sensor.

What to check

Now try it yourselves.

- Don't add too many batteries at once! You will blow the bulb.
- How will you decide how bright the bulbs are or how loud the buzzer is?

What did you find?

Zafar decided to use two batteries in a circuit and to keep adding bulbs to see what happened. He put his results in a table.

Number of bulbs	Brightness
1	extremely bright
2	bright
3	dim
4	very dim
5	can't see any light

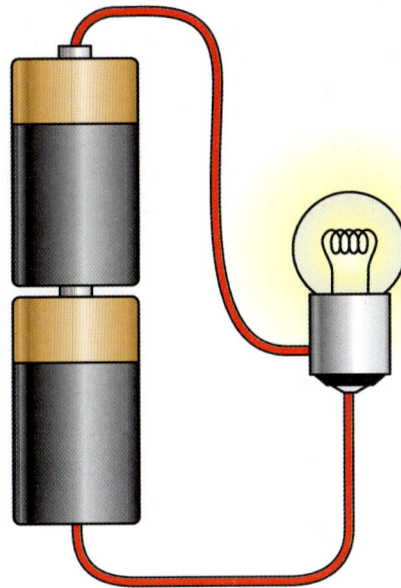

Two batteries make a bulb brighter

- Draw a chart of your results or use Zafar's. If you have a light sensor on your computer use it to make more accurate measurements. You could plot these results on a bar graph.

- When were the bulbs brightest? When were they dimmest? Why do you think that was? Were all the bulbs in the circuit equally dim or equally bright? Why was that?

Can you do better?

- Why should you only make one change at a time?
- Did you ever make more than one change? What's wrong with that?

Now predict

Zafar had space to put two batteries in his model. He connected the bulbs to them and was happy with how bright they were. When he connected the buzzer the lights went dimmer again. The buzzer worked all the time the lights were on.

- How can Zafar have two bright bulbs and a buzzer he can turn on and off, using just two batteries?
- How can Zafar make an electric motor go faster and slower?

Magnets and metals

Things to learn
- There are forces between magnets.
- Magnets can attract and repel each other.
- Magnets attract some metals but not others.

An invisible force

A magnet is a piece of iron or steel with an invisible **force**. It can attract or pull some metals. Magnets can attract or repel other magnets. Only a magnet can repel or push another magnet.

The ends of magnets are called poles. Each magnet has a north and a south pole. North and south poles attract. But north poles repel north poles. South poles repel south poles.

Magnetic metals

Not all metals are magnetic. Iron is a magnetic metal. It is attracted to a magnet. Steel is made from iron. Steel is magnetic. Nickel and cobalt are not as common as iron and steel. But nickel and cobalt are magnetic, too.

Do you know other metals such as copper and aluminium, gold and silver, tin and zinc? They are all metals, but they are not magnetic!

Shiny stainless steel is used to make knives and forks. Strangely, steel is magnetic, but stainless steel is not.

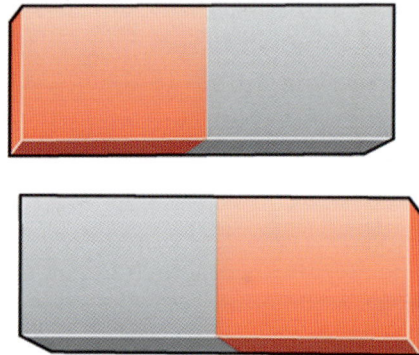

Earth's poles

Planet Earth has magnetic poles. The Earth's magnetic force is strongest at the poles. A compass has a magnet that is free to turn. The compass needle lines up with the Earth's magnetic poles. A compass helps you find your way.

Things to do

Push and pull

Mark the poles of a bar magnet 'N' and 'S' for north and south.

- Use it to find the north and south poles of other magnets.
- Do horseshoe magnets have poles?
- Do button and ring magnets have poles?
- Test magnets in other shapes. Find their poles.

Metal testing

Test safe metal objects in the room. Are they magnetic? What metal do you think they are made from?

DO NOT test electrical devices, watches or cards with black strips!

Dig deeper

Find out:
- how electricity generators work. Electricity generators contain magnets. When you make the magnets move – using a steam turbine, moving water or the power of the wind – you generate electricity.

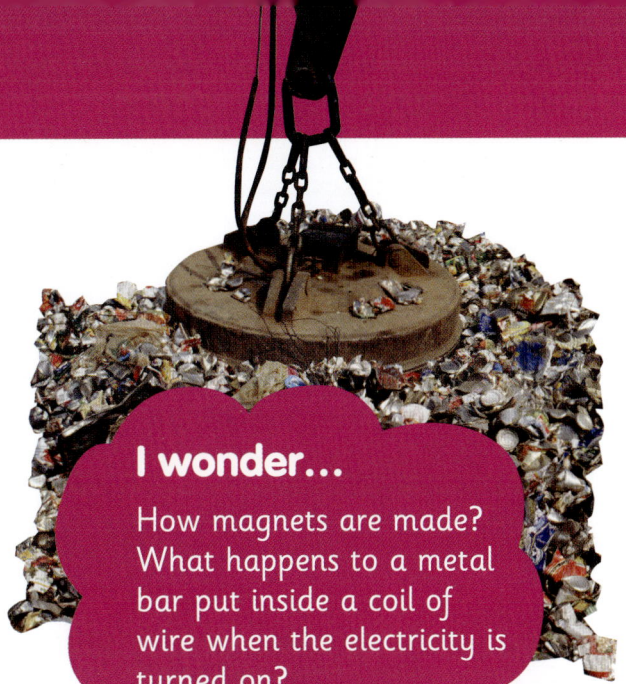

I wonder...

How magnets are made? What happens to a metal bar put inside a coil of wire when the electricity is turned on?

Did you know?

- A magnetic field is invisible. It can work through some other objects. You can make something magnetic move on a table top by attracting it with a magnet underneath the table. You can make it stick to the bottom of the table. Put a magnet on the table top. The magnetic field works through the table.
- An electromagnet is a magnet you can switch on and off. An electromagnet without electricity is just a metal bar in a coil of wire. But switch it on and it becomes a powerful magnet. It can lift scrap metal, ring doorbells or pull a steel splinter from your eye.

What have you learned? ✔

- You know the difference between electricity from batteries and mains electricity.
- You can construct a simple circuit.
- You can say why some simple circuits will work and others will not.
- You know what an electrical conductor is and you can name some.
- You know what an electrical insulator is and you can name some.
- You know how electricity travels in a circuit.
- You can construct a switch.
- You can explain how to change the brightness of bulbs.
- You can describe what might happen in a circuit if the components are not matched.
- You know that magnets can attract or repel each other.
- You know that magnets attract some metals but not others.

Find out more about...

- how a bicycle dynamo can generate electricity
- how a dimmer switch works.

Check-up

Yunis has made a circuit using two batteries, a bulb and a motor but it doesn't work.

Think of as many reasons as you can to explain why the circuit might not work.

The answer!

Remember that light on the landing? Do you switch it on to go downstairs on a dark morning? Do you turn it off before you go out? How does that work? Well, you only need one source of electricity. But those two switches need to be in separate circuits. The electricity needs two different paths to the bulb.
Try it with a bulb, a battery and two switches. Can you make it work?

Unit 7: Sound

'Turn that dreadful noise down, please!' Has anyone ever said that to you? Noise is sound that we don't like. What's noisy to one person may be music to someone else! Sound surrounds us. Even when we think it's quiet we can still hear the sound of our own breathing or wind **rustling** through trees. Sound can make us laugh or cry; it can even **shatter** glass!

What do you know?

- Hearing is one of your five senses.
- Sounds come from a distance.
- Sounds can be produced in different ways.
- Sounds can be loud or quiet.
- There are high sounds and low sounds.
- The sounds made by musical instruments can be changed.

Words to learn

high	soft
loud	tension
loudness	tune
low	vibrate
muffle	volume
pitch	wave

Skills check

Can you...

- make careful observations and measurements?
- collect evidence and see how good it is?
- explain what you've found out?
- predict something you don't yet know?

Let's find out…

Tariq's brother bought him a drum kit for his birthday. Tariq is delighted and plays it every night. Tariq's mum is not so happy. She thinks it's far too noisy and is worried about disturbing the neighbours. She's told Tariq that if he can't make the drums quieter, the drum kit will have to go. What can he do?

Making sounds

Sound vibrations

Sound is energy that we can hear. Sounds are made when a moving object makes the air vibrate. A sound travels from its source through the air in invisible **waves** until it reaches our ears. Our ears pick up the **vibrations**. We turn these into signals our brain understands as sound. How many sounds can you hear right now? Where are the sounds coming from?

Spreading sounds

Sound waves are like the **ripples** on a pond. They spread out in all directions. These sounds travel to us. Then we can hear them.

Sounds spread up and down too. Sound energy passes from one air particle to the next until it reaches us.

The closer you are to the source of the sound, the more energy it has and the louder it is. The further away from the source, the quieter the noise.

Sound travels

Sound can travel through all sorts of materials. Solid wood and metal conduct sound, and so do liquids. Whales 'sing' to each other through hundreds of kilometres of water.

Things to do

See the sound

When something is hit, **plucked** or **twanged** it may vibrate and make a sound. Normally, we can't see sound. But we can see and feel some vibrations.

Try these:

- Put your fingers on your throat. Start talking or singing. What can you feel?
- Hold a ruler so it hangs over the edge of a table. Push down on the free end and let go. Can you see the vibrations and hear the twang?
- Strike a **tuning fork**. Gently touch the surface of water in a bowl with the vibrating **prongs**. Can you make a splash?

Dig deeper

Find out:
- how our ears work and how we can protect them
- how we hear sounds
- how we measure sound in **decibels**.

Very loud noises can damage your ears.

I wonder...

In a thunderstorm, why do we see the lightning before we hear the thunder?

Did you know?

- Sound travels in air at around 340 metres per second. It travels faster if the air is warm.
- The furthest the human voice has travelled without using a microphone is 17 km.

How sound travels

Your challenge
● Identify materials that sound travels through.
● Plan a fair test.

I'm bored! I never thought I'd miss going to school.

Yes. It's funny. We can't see school, but we can hear our friends playing. Why is that?

I know. It makes it worse hearing everyone at playtime.

Jain and Sayed have **chicken pox**. They must stay off school for a while.

What to do

Listen carefully to the sounds you can hear around you. Some might be from outside your classroom. What materials have they travelled through before you hear them? Do we have to see something to hear it?

Jain and Sayed decided to find out what materials sound travelled through. They filled sandwich bags with different materials. How well could they hear their alarm clock ticking through each bag?

What you need
● Different materials like cotton wool, wood, water
● Sandwich bags
● A clock or watch that ticks.

What to check

Now try it yourselves.
● What will you put in your bags?
● How will you decide how loud the clock ticks?
● Does it matter who listens?
● How can you keep the quantities of your materials the same? Does it matter?

Material	Volume of sound
air	quiet
water	loud
cotton wool	quite quiet
wood	really loud

What did you find?

Sound travelled through all the materials that the children tested. Some were better than others. Here are their results:

We could wrap a clock in different materials and see if we could hear it.

I think we should try to make a **soundproof** box.

How about making a hat or ear-muffs from different things and seeing how much we can hear?

- The children were puzzled. It seemed that sound travelled poorly through air!
- Why do you think the children got these results? Are they the same as yours?

Can you do better?

- How good is your evidence?
- Can you think of a general rule?
- How could Jain and Sayed use their computer to improve their results?
- Which is the best way to describe how loud or quiet a sound is?

Now predict

- The children knew that sound travels as vibrations. The vibrations are passed from particle to particle. The particles in solids are closer together than those in liquids. The particles in liquids are closer together than those in gases.
- The closer together the particles were in the material tested, the better the sound travelled through it. What would happen if they didn't put their ear directly onto the bag but moved further away from it? Would the sound be louder or quieter? Why?

Muffling sound

Your challenge

- Find which materials muffle sound best.
- Find which materials reflect sound better than others.
- Plan a fair test.
- Decide what evidence to collect.

Ali is having his bedroom re-decorated.

Everything sounds so much louder in here! The sound seems to be **echoing**.

It'll be quieter with the curtains up and the carpet laid.

What you need

- A clock or **metronome**
- Different materials like newspaper, felt, cotton wool, bubble wrap, **polystyrene**, foam
- Two boxes with lids.

What to do

Ali thought about what Dad had said. In school, his footsteps sounded louder on the hard floor of the gym than on the classroom carpet. The carpet **muffled** the sound. Ali and his friends decided to find which materials muffled sound the most.

What to check

Now try it yourselves.

- How will you keep your test fair?
- What are you going to measure?
- How will you decide how loud the sound is?
- Will you need any special equipment to measure the sound?
- How much soundproofing material will you use?

What did you find?

Ali made an insulated box. He put a ticking metronome inside it. He used a sound sensor to measure the level of sound outside the box. First, he measured the ticking with no **soundproofing** material. Why? He changed the soundproofing materials. Then he measured from the same distance away from the box each time. He wrote down what he heard. He recorded his results in a spreadsheet.

● Draw a chart of your results or use Ali's. What was the best material to muffle the sound? Which was the least **effective**? Think of reasons why. Remember that sound is absorbed by **soft** carpets.

Test material	Sound heard
no soundproofing	loud
scrunched up newspaper	quite loud
one layer of felt	soft
sheet of bubble wrap	quite loud
carpet	quiet
foam	very soft
polystyrene shapes	soft
cotton wool	very soft

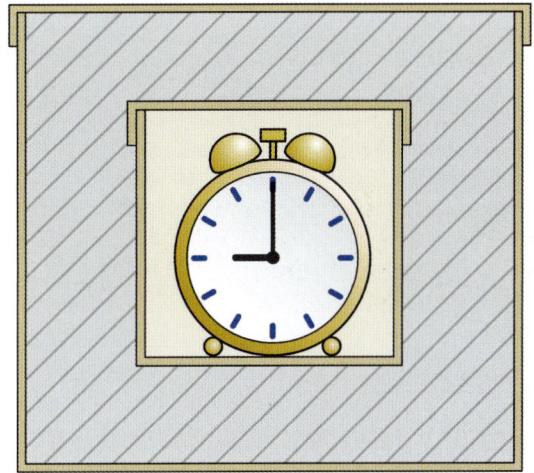

Soundproofed box

Can you do better?

● How good is your evidence?
● What other materials can you find to test?
● When is it important to muffle sound?

Now predict

● Imagine you are organizing a party in the school gym. You want the music to be loud enough to enjoy. You don't want to turn the volume down. What could you do to make sure the noise stays inside the party?

Pitch and volume

Things to learn

- Volume describes how loud a sound is.
- Pitch describes how high or low a sound is.
- The pitch of a string depends on its length and thickness.
- The pitch and loudness of an instrument can be changed.

Different sounds

Vibrations made by blowing, striking, plucking or stroking something produce most sounds. If you change the way you make vibrations, you can change the sound.

The **loudness** of a drum is altered by how hard it is hit.

If you hit it very hard, you make big vibrations on the drum skin. This makes a **loud** sound or **volume**. Hit a drum gently and you'll get a quieter sound. Try it!

High or low?

We call how **high** or **low** a sound is the **pitch**. The pitch is the speed of the sound's vibration. If you change the length or size of the vibrating object, you can change the pitch of the sound. A small or short instrument vibrates very quickly and gives a high note. A large or long instrument vibrates more slowly and gives a lower note. That's why a violin has a higher pitch than a double bass.

Different-sized drums produce different notes, too — the bigger the drum, the lower or deeper the note. You can change the pitch of a string by altering its **tension**, making it tighter or looser. A loose string gives a lower note than a tight string.

Dogs and cats have very senstive hearing

Things to do

Pitch-pipes

Look at the mouthpiece of a clarinet. There is a wooden **reed** that vibrates and produces a sound when it's blown into.

- Make one by cutting a 'Λ' shape into the end of a drinking straw. Close your lips around the end of the straw. As you blow into it you should produce a note. In between each blow, carefully cut the end of your straw 1 cm shorter. What happens to the pitch? Why?

Changing pitch

Your challenge

● Find out how to change the pitch of a string.

Which do you think makes the higher sound – a trombone or a trumpet? Why?

The cello is bigger than the oud and it has longer strings. It makes a lower sound.

A group of visiting musicians are talking to Class 4.

The short strings on my oud make a high sound.

What to do

The students decided to investigate the stringed instruments. They wanted to discover ways to change the pitch of a string. Here are their ideas:

I'm going to twang elastic bands. I think the thicker ones will sound lower than the thin ones.

I'll shorten an elastic band by sliding a ruler along it.

I'm going to add weights to the end of a string and see what happens.

What you need

● A paper cup
● Thin string
● Sticky tape
● A ruler
● Paper clips
● Elastic bands
● Plastic tubs
● A tape recorder or video camera
● Weights.

What to check

Now try it yourselves.

● What are you going to change?
● What needs to stay the same?
● How will you decide what is a low or a high sound?
● How will you compare your results with other people's?

What did you find?

Omar and Yasmin made a model of a guitar neck.

They put a paper cup at the end to help make the sound louder. First they plucked the open string and used this sound as their starting point. Then they made the string shorter by about 2 cm each time. They made a graph of their investigation. It looked like this:

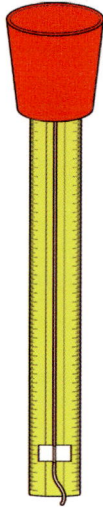

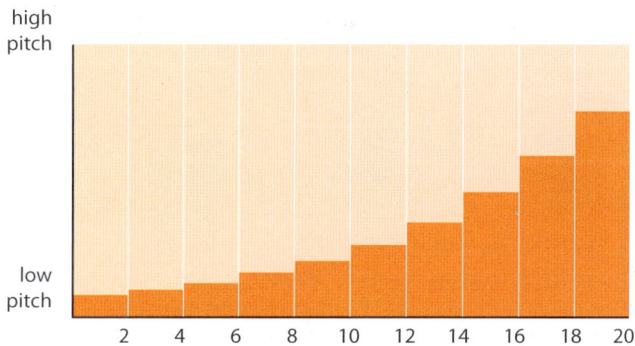

string shortened by 2cm each time

- Draw a chart of your results. What was the lowest sound you could make? What was the highest sound?
- Make a general rule about how to change the pitch of a string.

Can you do better?

- How good is your evidence?
- If you did this investigation again, is there anything you would change or do differently?
- What would happen if you used different types of string?
- How thick do your strings need to be?

Now predict

- At the end of the day, the musicians gave a concert in the school hall. Before they started to play they needed to tune their instruments. They changed the note of each one. How would each musician tune their instrument?

Different instruments

Things to learn

- A column of air in a wind instrument vibrates to give a sound.
- The pitch of a wind instrument can be changed.
- Changing the length of the column of air changes the pitch.

Tubular tones

Trumpets, clarinets, pipes, saxophones, recorders and even kazoos all work because air vibrates inside a tube. As the air bounces down the tube it makes a sound. The shorter the tube, the higher the pitch of the note we hear. A long tube gives a lower note.

Look at a recorder or other wind instrument. How does it make a note? Play a high note. Now play a low note. What did you have to do to change the pitch? What was vibrating in the recorder? How did this change when you changed the note? Draw a diagram of what's happening inside the recorder when you play a note.

A bass recorder plays lower notes than a descant recorder

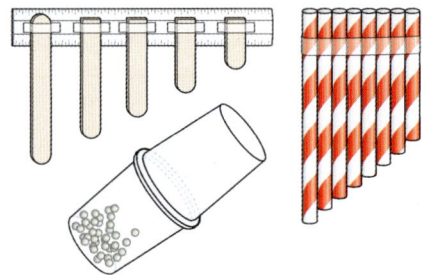

Junk box band

Look at these pictures of home-made instruments. What sounds do these instruments make? Which part of each instrument makes the sound?

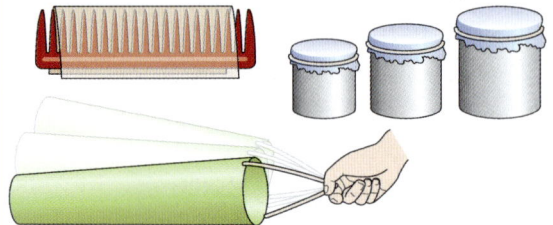

What sound can you make if you blow into an empty bottle?

I wonder...

Can we call the human voice an instrument? How do we make sounds with our voices?

Things to do

Bottle organ

Some instruments, like flutes, need air blown across the top of a tube to make a sound. If you cover up the air holes with your fingers, you can change the length of the vibrating column of air inside and change the pitch of the note.

- You can make columns of air vibrate by blowing across the top of an empty glass bottle.
- You can make a tune with several bottles. Collect identical glass bottles and line them up. Change the pitch of the sound by adding different amounts of water to each bottle. Can you make a scale?
- Which bottle gives the highest note? Which bottle gives the lowest note? What is vibrating to make the sound?

Dig deeper

Find out:
- about the different ways that light and sound travel.

Did you know?

- Sound can hurt you. Loud noises injure your ears. Very loud sounds can break the bones in your ear.
- The loudest known noise was the eruption of the Krakatoa volcano off the coast of Sumatra in 1883. The sound could be heard an incredible 5000 km away.

What have you learned?

- There are many different types of sound.
- Sounds are made when objects vibrate.
- A sound always has a source.
- Sound can travel through solids, liquids and gases.
- Most sounds we hear have travelled through air.
- Sound travels in waves.
- The louder a sound, the more energy it has.
- Sound travels in all directions from its source.
- The closer we are to the source of a sound, the louder it is.
- Loudness is measured in decibels.
- Some materials muffle sounds.
- Sound can bounce off hard, smooth surfaces.
- The pitch of a sound is how low or high it is.

Find out more about...

- how animals make sounds with their voices.

Check-up

Hannah's baby sister has been playing with Hannah's guitar. She's loosened all the strings and it's completely out of **tune**. What does Hannah need to do to tune her guitar? How will she know if the notes are correct?

The answer!

Do you remember the question about Tariq's drum kit?

To make the sounds quieter, Tariq could use cork practice mats and softer tipped drumsticks to reduce the vibrations of the drum skin. He could also hit his drums a little less hard!

To stop the sounds travelling he could soundproof his room with heavy curtains, cushions and soft furnishings. These would all absorb sounds. Tariq should stand his drum kit on a thick rug to help stop the sound travelling downwards, too.

What do you know?
- Think about these statements.
- Which do you know? Which can you do?

- I have learned to name the parts of my body – knee, elbow, wrist, thigh, etc.
- I can tell you what I observe when I do things.
- I know that bones grow as an animal grows.
- I have learned to make observations about which bones are biggest.
- I have learned how to group bones by size.
- I have learned to make observations about how bone feels and looks.
- I know why we have a skeleton and muscles.
- I have learned to explain why muscles change shape as I move.
- I have learned to measure the length of people's limbs.
- I have learned to explain how joints work.
- I know that muscles work in pairs: when one muscle contracts the other relaxes.
- I know that when I investigate I can only change one factor at a time – the people I measure, for example.
- I know how to relate my conclusion to my prediction and use scientific language.
- I know that different medicines can be given in different ways to make you feel better.
- I know that a drug is a substance that affects the way our body works.
- I know that medicines are types of drugs.

Unit 2: Living things in their environment checklist

What do you know?
- Think about these statements.
- Which do you know? Which can you do?

- I can describe an animal or plant.
- I can tell you what I observe.
- I have learned the conditions that animals and plants need to survive.
- I know that different animals and plants are found in different places.
- I have learned to place animals and plants into groups.
- I am learning how to make and record regular observations of my habitats.
- I can explain how an animal, such as a camel or a penguin, is adapted to its environment.
- I can explain why an animal or plant has adapted to suit its environment.
- I can explain why small invertebrates chose similar places in my investigation.
- I have learned how to use a branching key to identify animals and plants.
- I have learned to use a food chain to describe a feeding relationship.
- I can suggest ways I could improve my habitat investigations.
- I have learned some ways that human activity affects the environment.

Unit 3: Keeping warm checklist

What do you know?

- Think about these statements.
- Which do you know? Which can you do?

- I can describe some thermal conductors and insulator.
- I can tell you what I observe.
- I have learned to identify a range of materials, like wood, plastic and metal.
- I have learned to group materials on how good they are as thermal insulators.
- I can make and record regular observations of cooling and warming.
- I have learned to use a stopwatch.
- I know why saucepans are made from a conductor and the handle is made from an insulator.
- I can explain which insulation keeps water warmest and ice coldest.
- I have learned to measure temperature accurately.
- I know that a hot drink will cool to room temperature in time.
- I have learned to keep my investigations fair, by only changing one factor at a time.
- I have learned to plot a bar chart of my results.

Unit 4: Separating solids and liquids checklist

What do you know?
- Think about these statements.
- Which do you know? Which can you do?

- I can explain the differences between ice and water.
- I can list some differences between solids and liquids, and give you some examples.
- I have learned to sort familiar materials into solids and liquids and give you reasons.
- I can tell you what happens to ice if you heat it or water if you cool it.
- I can tell you what happens to water when it evaporates.
- I have learned to sort unfamiliar materials into groups and give you reasons for my decisions.
- I know that changes to ice and water can be reversed.
- I know how sieves work and can explain how a filter is like a fine sieve.
- I can tell you how the differences between materials can be used to group them as solids or liquids.
- I can explain filtering and evaporation.

Unit 5: Gases around us checklist

What do you know?
- Think about these statements.
- Which do you know? Which can you do?

- I can name some familiar gases.
- I can tell you what I observe.
- I can tell you about a range of gases, like air, carbon dioxide and hydrogen.
- I have learned to use a stopwatch.
- I know that gases move from place to place.
- I have learned to measure the volume of a liquid.
- I know that there are many different gases.
- I know that a liquid evaporates to form a vapour.
- I know when to repeat my observations and measurements.
- I have learned to plot a bar chart of my results.
- I have learned to describe the difference between the properties of solids, liquids and gases.
- I have learned to describe how a liquid and a gas are related.
- I have learned to recognize when evaporation is taking place in different everyday contexts.
- I can explain why I should repeat measurements and observations.

What do you know?

- Think about these statements.
- Which do you know? Which can you do?

- I can show you how to make a simple circuit, either by describing it to you or by drawing a picture.
- I have learned to make up a simple circuit and explain what I have done.
- I have learned to use electrical components to make up simple circuits and tell you whether my predictions about them were correct.
- I have learned to compare the way that bulbs work in different electrical circuits.
- I have learned to carry out a fair test – of insulators and conductors, or of changes in an electrical circuit – and suggest ways of doing it better.
- I can explain to you why a bulb does not light – that there is a break in the circuit or that the switch is open.
- I have learned to choose components to add to my circuits, predict what they will do and explain what happened when I added them.
- I can tell you how to put a bulb into an electric circuit and how to control it with a switch.

What do you know?
- Think about these statements.
- Which do you know? Which can you do?

- I know that there are many different sound sources and I can name some.
- I can tell you about my observations of changing sounds.
- I can describe the differences between different sounds in terms of volume and pitch.
- I know that sound travels through different materials to my ears.
- I can describe my discoveries about musical instruments.
- I can explain how changing the length or tension of a string, for example, changes the pitch or volume of a note.
- I can generalize about changes in sound – for example, the tighter the string, the higher the note.
- I have learned to observe and record differences in volume and pitch.
- I can show you what is vibrating in a musical instrument.
- I can tell you how sound travels – and why it travels better through solids than through gases.
- I can make changes to sounds and record how I did it. I can link my discoveries to my understanding of how sound travels.
- I can explain how sound waves are made and how they travel, and how they differ in shape with pitch and volume.
- I can plan and carry out a full investigation into changing pitch or volume, record and graph my results. I can suggest ways of getting a better result next time.

Glossary

adapted – an animal or a plant that has changed to suit its environment

air – the gas around us; a mixture of oxygen, nitrogen and carbon dioxide

alter – change

anaesthetic – a drug that stops you feeling pain

astronomer – a scientist who studies the stars and planets

backbone – the long bone in the back made up of many smaller bones

battery – a device that pushes electricity round a circuit

bird's-eye view – a view of something from high above it

break – gap in a circuit

bulb – contains a fine wire that glows to emit light

buzzer – an electrical component that vibrates noisily

capillary action – the force that makes a liquid rise up a narrow tube

carbon dioxide – waste gas from body processes

cell – one cylindrical unit of a battery; it pushes electricity round a circuit

Celsius – a temperature scale

centipede – a small invertebrate with one pair of legs to each segment

change of state – from solid to liquid, for example

chicken pox – an infectious illness that causes a slight fever and spots on your skin

chlorine – yellow-green gas with a strong smell

circuit – path of electricity

classification – sorting things into groups

component – one of several parts that together make up a whole machine, system, etc.

condition – the state in which animals and plants live

conduct – transmit heat, sound or electricity

conductor – a material that transmits heat, sound or electricity easily

consumer – an animal or a plant that eats other animals or plants

contract – become smaller or shorter

cordial – sweet fruit juice that you add water to before you drink it

core – the central part of something

current – the electricity that flows round a circuit

decibel (dB) – the unit of measurement of the volume of sound

degree – a unit of temperature

delicate – easily damaged or broken

detect – notice or discover something, especially something that is not easy to see or hear

diagram – simple picture

dim – a low light

disperse – spread in different directions

dispose – get rid of, or throw away

dissolve – when a solid mixes with a liquid and the mixture looks clear

disturb – change a normal situation in a way that causes problems

drug - any substance which changes the way our body works

dump – get rid of something that you do not want

echo – sound bounced from a hard surface

effective – successful

energy efficient – without wasting energy

environment – our general surroundings

evaporation – the change of state from liquid to gas

evolution – gradual change or growth into a different form

expand – get bigger

fertilizer – a substance (often chemical) that is put on the soil to make plants grow

fibre – a thin thread or one of the thin parts like threads that form natural materials

filtering – separating a solid from a liquid or gas with a fine sieve

flat – a drink that is flat has no bubbles of gas in it

flexible – bendy or pliable material

flowing – hanging or moving in a smooth graceful way

fluffy – very light and soft to touch

fluorescent – a fluorescent tube is filled with gas, which shines with a bright light when electricity is passed through it

food chain – the flow of energy from the Sun through a green plant and animals

force – a push or a pull

forearm – the lower part of the arm between the wrist and the elbow

gas – free flowing material that fills any space and has weight but no shape

gunpowder – an explosive substance used in bombs and fireworks

habit – something that you do regularly or usually

habitat – the natural home of an animal or plant

heat – energy when it is tranferred from one form to another

helium – light gas used in balloons

high – sound made by rapid vibrations; not deep or low

honeycomb – a structure made by bees, which consists of many six-sided cells, or something that is arranged or shaped in this pattern

hydraulic – moved or operated by the pressure of water or other liquid

hydrogen – flammable gas

ice lolly – sweet–tasting ice on a stick

identity – what something is

inflate – fill something with air or gas so that it becomes larger

inhale – to breathe in

insoluble – a solid that does not dissolve in a liquid

insulation – material that slows or stops heat, sound or electricity

internal – inside a person, place or object

invertebrate – a creature without a backbone

irreversible – cannot change back to how it was before

jolt – a sudden shock

junk – old or unwanted objects

key – a means to help identify something or someone

knuckles – the joints in your fingers, including the ones where your fingers join your hands

krill – small shellfish

landing – the floor at the top of a set of stairs or between two sets of stairs

lead (pencil) – the central part of a pencil that makes marks made of carbon or graphite

lentil – a small round seed like a bean, dried and used for food

liquid – a material that flows into a container to make a flat surface

loft – a room or space under the roof of a building

loud – strong sound made by a large or noisy instrument

loudness – measure of noise or sound

low – sound made by slow vibrations; not high or shrill

lubrication – using a material such as oil to make something move more smoothly

lump – small piece of something solid, without a particular shape

mammal – an animal with hair that gives birth to a live baby and feeds its young with milk from the mother's body

marrow – the soft fatty substance in the hollow centre of bones

matter – the stuff everything is made from

medicine – a drug we take to treat illness

melt – to change from solid to liquid when warm

metronome – a piece of equipment that makes a regular repeated sound like a clock, showing the speed at which music should be played

mercury – a heavy silver–white poisonous metal that is liquid at ordinary temperatures

molecule – the smallest unit into which many substances can be divided without losing its own chemical nature, usually consisting of two or more atoms

muffle – to quieten or deaden sound

muscle – body tissue that can contract and pull – but not expand or push

odourless – having no smell

offspring – children or baby animals

organism – individual living thing, such as a plant or animal

oxygen – gas essential for living processes and burning

particles – small pieces

petri dish – small clear dish with a cover used by scientists, especially for growing bacteria

pips – small seeds from fruit such as an apple or orange

pitch – speed of vibration and level of sound

plaster cast – a cover made from plaster of Paris, put around an arm, leg, etc. to keep a broken bone in place while it mends

pluck – to pull something quickly to remove it or make a noise

pollutant – a substance that makes air, water or soil, etc. dirty

pollution – the process of making air, water, soil, etc. dirty and not suitable for people to use

polystyrene – a soft light plastic material that prevents heat or cold from passing through it, used especially for making containers

predator – an animal that eats another animal for food

prevent – stop something from happening

prey – an animal that is eaten by a predator

producer – provides food for animals; almost always a green plant

prong – a thin sharp point of something such as a fork

protects – keeps safe from harm

pulp – a very soft substance that is almost liquid, made by crushing plants, wood, vegetables etc.

recover – to get better

reed – thin piece of wood attached to the mouthpiece of a musical instrument that produces a sound when you blow over it

relax – muscle not contracting and so getting bigger or longer

remedy – a medicine to cure an illness or pain that is not serious

renewable energy – energy such as solar or wind energy that is replaced naturally

residue – a substance that remains on a surface or in a container or that remains after a chemical process

reversed – changed back

ribs – bony cage that protects the body organs and moves for breathing

ripple – small low waves on the surface of a liquid

rustling – the noise made as leaves rub up against each other

separate – set things apart or remove something from a mixture

sewage – the mixture of waste from the human body and used water carried away from houses by pipes under the ground

shatter – break suddenly into small pieces

shell – a hard protective covering

shelter – a place to live where you are protected from the weather and danger

shrimp – a small sea creature with a shell, ten legs and a tail

shrub – a small bush with several woody stems

sieve – used to separate solids from liquids

skeleton – the framework of bones in your body

skull – bony protection for the brain

soft – not hard or firm, or a gentle sound

solid – a material that keeps its shape, however small

solidify – to become solid

soluble – any solid or gas that dissolves in a liquid

solution – a liquid with something dissolved in it

soundproof – sound cannot pass through it

splinter – break into thin sharp pieces

spongy – soft and full of holes that contain air or liquid

spy – someone whose job is to find out secret information

squidgy – soft and easy to press

switch – makes and breaks a circuit

syringe – an instrument for taking blood from someone's body or putting liquid, drugs, etc. into it. A hollow plastic tube and needle

temperature – measure of how hot something is

tendons – strong tissue that joins the muscles to the bones at the joints

tension – tightness

terminal – part of an electrical device through which electricity enters or leaves

thermal – involving heat

thermometer – instrument to measure temperature

tune – to make a musical instrument harmonious

tuning fork – a small U-shaped steel instrument that makes a particular musical note when you hit it

twang – making a ringing sound by pulling and letting go

twig – a small, very thin stem of wood that grows from branches on a tree

vacuum – a space empty of all gas

vertebrate – a creature with a backbone

vibration – rapid movement from side to side

voltage – the force of an electrical current measured in volts

volume – level of sound

waste products – useless materials or substances

water vapour – a mass of very small drops of water which float in the air, product of evaporation

wave – movement of a liquid

wiggle – move with small movements from side to side or up and down

wild – something that gows or lives in nature

Index

air 62–7, 90
air-conditioning 39
alchemists 49
amphibians 28
anaesthetics 69
astronauts 8
atmosphere 65
atoms 48, 76

batteries 77, 79, 84–5
bones 1–9
bulbs 78, 80, 84–5

Celsius scale 34, 37
circuits 78–9
classification 21
containers 39, 42–3
cooling 39, 56–7
current 76
cylinders 68

desert habitats 18, 19
dissolving solids 56, 58–9
drugs 14–15

echo 94, 97
electricity 75–88
electrons 76, 77
energy 26–7
environments 17–32
evaporation 70–1
evolution 23
exercise 12–13

Fahrenheit scale 34, 37
fat 45
fertilizers 30
filters 54, 55
flasks 42
fluorescent lights 68
food 26–7, 39, 52–3, 66, 70

force 86–7
fur 45

Galileo 35
gases 47, 61–74
grasses 20
gravity 8
growth 6–7
gunpowder 55

habitats 17–32
hair 55
hearing 34, 89–102
heart 12, 13
hinge joints 4, 10

ice 38, 40, 41, 56, 72
insects 9, 11, 24, 67
instruments 96–101
insulation 33, 42–4, 80
invertebrates 9, 24–5, 67

keys 22–3

lava 56
lights 68, 78, 80, 84–5
liquids 35–6, 47–60, 72–3
loudness 96–7

magnets 86–7
mammals 20
marrow 4, 9
mass 63
materials 33, 52–5, 92–3
matter 47–60, 64, 72–3
medicine 14–15
melting 40
metals 42, 49, 86–7
metronomes 94
muffling sound 94–5
muscles 10–13

oceans 19
oxygen 68

pitch 96–7, 98–9
plants 20, 21, 26
plastic cups 42–3
polar bears 45
pollution 30
polystyrene 94
pond weeds 23
predators 26, 27
prey 26
producers 26
pull/push forces 87

recycling 29, 31
room temperature 36

salts 57
sand 65
saucepans 45
seaweeds 23
senses 34, 70, 89–102
sewage 30
sharks 27
shells 2
shrubs 20
sieves 54, 55
silver 86
skeletons 1–9
skunks 20
slugs 9
smell 34, 70
snails 9
snakes 3
soil 66–7
solids 47–60, 72–3
solution 56
sound 89–102
space 8, 65
states of matter 72–3
steam 72

stringed instruments 96, 98–9
sugar 56
switches 82–3

taste 34
temperature 33–46, 56–7
terminals 77
thermometers 34, 35, 37
tigers 28
tin 86
tomatoes 23
tone 100
touch 34–5
trees 15, 20
tuning forks 91

ultrasound 97
underwear 44

vacuum 5, 42
vapour 56, 72
vibrations 90, 91
volcanoes 56
Voltaic pile 77
volume 96–7

waste products 30
water 30, 49, 56, 57, 65, 72
waves 90
whales 27, 90
wind 62
world temperatures 38
worms 9, 24, 67

X-rays 4